Gracefully Broken

Franklin Hawkins Kornegay Pinkney Wilson

ISBN: 9781098506605

DEDICATION

To our brothers and sisters in the Lord who have experienced the breaking and victory that comes along with following Christ and have a desire to let the world know there is hope in Christ Jesus our Lord!

To all who have walked along our side as we have gone through these periods in our life. Thank you for listening, lending a hand, for all the hugs and for not allowing us to give up, give in or go away. We want you to know we did not buy into the lies of the enemy and will forever declare the devil cannot get what we've got!

Hebrews 4:12 - For the word of God is alive and powerful. It is sharper than the sharpest two-edged sword, cutting between soul and spirit, between joint and marrow. It exposes our innermost thoughts and desires.

CONTENTS

ACKNOWLEDGMENTS

We would like to express gratitude to Almighty God for His love and faithfulness towards us. We would like to thank all those who pray with us every week and provided support to the World Intercessory Network ministry in any manner, we appreciate you.

Special thanks to Christian Hardy for the cover design, pictures, and Akili Harris for your assistance in the layout of this book. God has blessed you both, and we are grateful to for the connection. We also want to express our thanks to Miss Patrece Escalera for being our model. We thank them both for bringing to life the vision we had.

Above all, we would like to thank the members of our families who continuously support and encourage us. Ministry requires an innumerable amount of sacrifices of family time, and we want them to know that we appreciate them for sharing us with the world.

INTRODUCTION

G racefully broken is a collection of stories written by Women of God who have victoriously walked through a variety of challenging situations in life. It is their heart's desire to not only give glory to God for the marvelous things He has done but to also inspire others both male and female to know the power of God that can deliver, protect and set them free from the traps of life. As you walk through the pages of this book, you may feel the hurt and pain from some of the situations they encountered, but you will also come away with the assurance that God is a healer, a deliverer, redeemer, savior, and King. Let us not forget the most significant thing, just as God opened His heart of love and hope to each of these women and brought them through in victory; He stands ready and willing to do the same for anyone who will open their heart and allow Him into their life.

CHAPTER 1

All You Need Is A Word From God

By Kimberly Pinkney

All You Need Is A Word From God

By Kimberly Pinkney

It was Valentine's Day 1992. I should have been happy, but my mind was consumed with one thought, and it involved my baby. Just a few months earlier, Robert had returned to Germany from a deployment to Kuwait, and a few days after that, we decided at the last minute to take a vacation to Georgia to see his family members, many of whom I had never met. The military flight took us to a base in Delaware, and from there, we took the bus to Florida and met one of Robert's sisters who drove us to Georgia. A couple of weeks later, we were back in Delaware awaiting a return flight to Germany. I began feeling a little nauseous, which prompted a visit to a doctor on the base that confirmed my suspicions that I was pregnant. The doctor set my due date to be September 15, and I was overjoyed! Back in Germany, our excitement about our impending new bundle of joy was palpable. We were filled with many new thoughts and ideas, not the least of which was wonderment about the gender of our baby.

Now less than two months later, I found myself in a hospital examination room where a doctor nonchalantly and unsympathetically announced the news of my miscarriage, handed me a piece of paper, and walked out of the room. There was no concern about my emotional well-being, no ascertaining of the availability of my

15

support system; just a thoughtless proclamation of the worst news I'd received up to that point, and a methodical moving on to the next person. I sat in that hospital room in shock and dismay, waiting for the nurse to come with the release papers to facilitate my checkout. All the anticipation and sharing of good news, and now, no baby. It was more than I thought I could take.

Robert was away in training, so his supervisor had driven me to the hospital and was now waiting for me in the lobby. We began the almost two-hour trek back to my house. For a few minutes, she did not say anything to me. I was glad because I would have immediately broken down, and I didn't want her to see me crying. After about ten minutes, she asked, in a sweet, compassionate voice, if there was anything she could do for me. I asked her to get my husband home. She was happy to oblige me.

On the return trip to the home base, my mind was assaulted continuously with inquiring, but rueful thoughts. I wondered why this had happened, what caused it to happen. I knew better than to blame God. So, I never questioned why God let this happen to me. I knew God had not caused my miscarriage. Yet, my mind was in a state of disarray because I simply did not understand, and I wanted my baby. I wanted to scream, holler, and cry out loud, but I wanted to wait until I got behind closed doors before venting my emotions. I was so deeply hurt with no one to comfort me at the moment. When we arrived at my house, I thanked the Sergeant for all she had done for me. Once inside my house, I made a beeline for the bathroom, closed the door, and got ready to scream why from the top of my lungs, but all that came out was Thank You, Jesus! And I screamed that over and over again. I stopped for a moment, thinking of how weird it was that I was praising God when I really just wanted recoil into a ball of self-pity. But before I realized it, I was again praising God, even more loudly.

The praise was coming from my spirit because my mind was overwhelmed with confusion and pain. In fact, from deep within my spirit - I cannot explain it - came this uncontrollable gushing of praise and thanksgiving. It was as if someone took over me. At the time, I did not know what was happening. Later, however, God told me that it was the Holy Spirit stepping in with intercession.

The Bible says, In the same way, the Spirit [comes to us and] helps us in our weakness. We do not know what prayer to offer or how to offer it as we should, but the Spirit Himself [knows our need and at the right time] intercedes on our behalf with sighs and groanings too deep for words (Romans 8:26 AMP). My Helper had stepped into that bathroom and given me the kind of help I truly needed.

Years later, I also realized that during that time of grief, sorrow, and hurt, Jesus Christ - that is, the Anointed One - used His Anointing - that is, the Holy Spirit - to heal my broken heart. After all, that is what scripture says: The Spirit of the Lord is upon Me because He…has sent Me to heal the brokenhearted (Luke 4:18 NKJV). Jesus wants to heal you as well from any hurts of the past or the present. He is the Anointed One, and He was sent to bring healing to anyone who calls out to him, and to any child of God who needs it.

I knew from prior teaching that when you are being attacked in your mind, one of the worst things you can do is to remain in complete silence, which has a way of opening the door to the enemy. To sit or brood in silence, when under demonic attack, only invites the enemy to exacerbate his attack, often through a barrage of words that push you further into depression and despair. I knew I had to fill my atmosphere with Word-based preaching that would counter the enemy's attack as well as provide answers to my situation. So, I searched through my selection of sermons and found just the right one to minister words of life to me and encourage me to praise God despite my feelings. I turned up the volume and selected auto-rewind so that it would play nonstop.

By this time, I had been up for over twenty-four hours, so with my blanket for comfort, I settled on my sofa. I was only able to listen to the preacher for about ten minutes before I fell soundly asleep. Over the next few hours, I would awake off and on, and remembering that I no longer carried a baby, I would start to cry. Then I would hear the voice of the preacher, extolling the goodness of God, encouraging me to praise God, and admonishing me to persevere. At that, I'd exchange my tears for praise until I'd fall asleep again. Every time the enemy wanted me to dwell on the negative, the Word I was hearing kept my mind focused on praising God.

The Apostle Paul says, Finally, believers, whatever is true, whatever is honorable and worthy of respect, whatever is right and confirmed by God's word, whatever is pure and wholesome, whatever is lovely and brings peace, whatever is admirable and of good repute; if there is any excellence, if there is anything worthy of praise, think continually on these things [center your mind on them, and implant them in your heart] (Philippians 4:8 AMP).

At all times, but especially in hard times, we would do well to order our thoughts and our heart according to Paul's injunction. And that is precisely what I did that night. I implanted the pure, delivering Word of God in my spirit and soul, letting the truth of His Word not only minister to me, but also pull me from darkness into His glorious light!

It is hard to think of praise and not think of I Thessalonians 5:18 (AMP): In every situation [no matter what the circumstances] be thankful and continually give thanks to God; for this is the will of God for you in Christ Jesus. Let me assure you, however, I was not thanking God for the miscarriage, nor was this scripture directing me to. I was thanking God in the situation, not for the situation, which means I was thanking and praising God in spite of the doctor's words announcing my miscarriage.

These days, I know how to praise God out of defeat and into victory. However, during that time, I had never faced such an ordeal, and it did not help that I was over five thousand miles from home, away from the wisdom and encouragement of my mother. So, praising God all alone in my house was definitely a challenge.

It was about six or seven o' clock in the evening when God awakened me with a question: What do you want from me? I told Him I wanted a baby by the end of the year, and

I received a definite impression from God that my request was granted. I fell back to sleep.

About an hour later, Robert's lieutenant called with news that Robert would be coming home that night. When Robert arrived, we hugged, and I cried some more. Later that week, I returned to the doctor for a checkup, and she informed me not to try to get pregnant again for at least a month. However, I did not listen to her instructions because I felt good physically, although I did not understand why.

Our lives gradually got back to normal, and the following month found me back in the doctor's office with a different doctor telling me I was pregnant, with a December due date. I was overjoyed and started laughing. I left the office, and God reminded me of that night when He promised to give me a baby by the end of the year. All I could think of was that God did it! God really did it! His Words do come to pass.

I thought of how Hannah prayed for a son and received a word from Eli that she could go in peace because God would grant her petition. Before that word from Eli, Hannah was distraught, barely able to go on. After the word from Eli, she wiped her tears and resumed relations with her husband. Eli's word brought Hannah peace and gave her the faith she needed to receive a baby from God.

I had heard a word from One greater than Eli, and just like God fulfilled His word to Hannah, He fulfilled His word to me. He gave me a healthy, approximately seven-pound baby girl on December 14 who loves God today and serves in our ministry. I often tell her she is my Hannah baby because God heard my cry and answered me. I want to encourage you to take some time and get a word from the Lord regarding your situation. You may be experiencing trouble in your marriage, with your child, on your job, in your home, or in some other part of your personal life. God has a word tailor-made for you that will bring you victory and deliverance. I want you to make yourself available to hear from Him and get the victory that rightfully belongs to you. How do you make yourself available to hear from God?

First, position yourself in the right atmosphere. Decide to block out all negative words or messages from people, television, the Internet, and social media. You need to feed on His Word instead. Put the Word of God in your mind. The heavier the situation, the more you need to hear the Word. In the natural, when you experience severe physical pain, you do not want a low-strength pain reliever; you want an extra-strength one. This is true as well with spiritual matters. You turn up your dose of God's Word, based on the intensity of your situation. Unlike natural medicine, you cannot overdose on the Word of God. So, take it, hear it, believe it, and receive it as much as you want. Play the Word while getting dressed in the morning, while at work, while driving home, while washing dishes, even while sleeping. This is how you position yourself to hear from God.

Second, learn to praise God whether you feel like it or not. I did not feel like praising God that day, but God knew that praise would bring Him into my situation where He could make the difference I desperately needed.

Consider Psalms 22:8 (AMP): You are holy, O You who are enthroned in [the holy place where] the praises of Israel [are offered]. We say it all the time in Church that the Lord inhabits the praises of His people. When praise goes forth, the presence and glory of God rest upon it, and He speaks, heals, delivers, provides, or does whatever is needed. Just as important, our praise is an expression of our gratitude and lets God know that we are thankful for His involvement in our lives and that our praise is not conditional. Therefore, never let the enemy keep you from opening your mouth and praising God during a troubled time.

Third, recognize the devil for the thief he is: The thief comes only to steal and kill and destroy. I came that they may have and enjoy life, and have it in abundance [to the full, till it overflows] (John 10:10 AMP). Here, Jesus lets us know that it is the enemy, and not God, who steals, kills, and destroys. And often, he kills and destroys by stealing the Word from us. He also likes to come at a moment of vulnerability, as he did when he tempted Jesus in the wilderness. This is precisely the reason that we must be sober [well balanced and self-disciplined…alert and cautious at all times [because our] enemy…prowls around like a roaring lion [fiercely hungry], seeking someone to devour (I Peter 5:8 AMP).

It was the enemy who came that day, trying to get me to blame God for something He did not do. But the Holy Spirit exposed him, and Jesus gave me a word (which I believed and expressed) that brought comfort, gladness, deliverance, peace, and nine months later, joy unspeakable and full of glory to God. In essence, the devil did not prevail! What are you facing right now as you read this book? I dare you to put it down for a quick moment and start praising God for healing, restoration, deliverance or whatever the need. Come on: do it now! When you do, you may hear something in your spirit, and if you do not hear something right away, just keep the Word of God going and your praise high, and your word will come.

Fourth, start expecting your deliverance to happen. I admonish you to let God start directing your steps into what to say or not to say, and what to do or not to do. When the doctor told Robert and me not to attempt impregnation for a month, something strong on the inside told me that we could try again in two weeks. Little did I know of the importance of this timing. God has a time for everything you need. Sometimes, we do not position ourselves to hear or obey His voice concerning that timing. If I had followed the doctor's voice, I would have run the risk of not having a baby by the end of the year, which is what God had promised me. There are times you need to heed the voices of doctors or other people, but not when you counter the voice of the Holy Spirit. That is an essential truth, but if you do not spend time with God, you might not be able to recognize Him when He speaks to you.

One final word: do not let the enemy cause you to abort your dreams, desires, wants, and needs. I was more on guard the next time I became pregnant. I was not in fear, but I listened to God's instructions. The enemy does not want you to give birth to your promises. There is a prime example of this in Numbers, chapters 13 & 14. God was ready to fulfill His promise to the Israelites and bring them into the Promised Land. He dispatched twelve spies to the land to bring back a report. He did not send them on a mission to ascertain if the Israelites could take the land. That had already been determined. He simply wanted them to report on the lay of the land and its resources. We pick up the story with the spies' report in Numbers 13 (NKJV).

> [27] Then they told him and said: "We went to the land where you sent us. It truly flows with milk and honey, and this is its fruit. [28] Nevertheless, the people who dwell in the land are strong; the cities are fortified and very large; moreover, we saw the descendants of Anak there. [29] The Amalekites dwell in the land of the South; the Hittites, the Jebusites, and the Amorites dwell in the mountains; and the Canaanites dwell by the sea and along the banks of the Jordan."

The devil will bring dream robbers or spiritual abortion doctors to tell you your dream is dead, that it's not looking right, or you're not strong enough, mature enough, saved enough, or right enough to have this dream or this promise. Even when people around you realize their dreams, the devil will do everything he can to deter you from fulfilling yours. But if you listen carefully, you will hear God encouraging you to go for it!

> [30] Then Caleb quieted the people before Moses, and said, "Let us go up at once and take possession, for we are well able to overcome it."

This is the kind of people we need to be and the kind of people we need surrounding us. You need to be a person who will not back down, a person who sees what God sees, who hears from God and obeys Him. A person who knows that God on the inside is greater than he that is in the world. You need to be like Caleb...like Joshua. But there will always be naysayers.

> [31] But the men who had gone up with him said, "We are not able to go up against the people, for they are stronger than we. "[32] And they gave the children of Israel a bad report of the land which they had spied out... [2] And all the children of Israel complained against Moses and Aaron, and the whole congregation said to them, "If only we had died in the land of Egypt! Or if only we had died in this wilderness! [3] Why has the Lord brought us to this land to fall by the sword, that our wives and children should become victims? Would it not be better for us to return to Egypt?"

Do not be ignorant of the devil's devices, which include negative reports that enslave people to fear and keep them from fulfilling the will of God. This is exactly what happened here. The negative report from the ten spies not only caused the Israelites to refuse to go to the Promised Land, but it also made them want to return to a land and a people that treated them so cruelly that they cried out to God for deliverance. Do not let this happen to you. When you know that God has spoken to you, stand your ground of faith and do not budge, even if everyone around you - including those you highly respect - see and talk things differently. Joshua and Caleb are exemplary examples to us in this regard.

Numbers 14:6-9 (NKJV):

> [6]But Joshua, the son of Nun and Caleb the son of Jephunneh, who were among those who had spied out the land, tore their clothes; [7]and they spoke to all the congregation of the children of Israel, saying: "The land we passed through to spy out is an exceedingly good land. [8]If the Lord delights in us, then He will bring us into this land and give it to us, 'a land which flows with milk and honey.' [9]Only do not rebel against the Lord, nor fear the people of the land, for they are our bread; their protection has departed from them, and the Lord is with us. Do not fear them."

Unfortunately, the Israelites did not heed the words of Joshua and Caleb, nor did they follow their faith. This resulted in their banishment into the wilderness until their death. They were on the very verge of walking into their destiny, but they instead let an evil report strike fear in their hearts and keep them out of the Promised Land. What a tragic tradeoff! Don't allow this happen to you! Remind yourself over and over again that fear has no place in your heart. There is only room for faith. You must, constantly meditate on II Timothy 1:7 (AMPC) until you are thoroughly divested of fear: God did not give us a spirit of timidity (of cowardice, of craven and cringing and fawning fear), but [He has given us a spirit] of power and of love and of calm and well-balanced mind and discipline and self-control. You will be like Joshua and Caleb, who were the only ones to reach their God-appointed destiny. They made it, not because they were privileged or gifted, but because they chose faith instead of fear. I have used these principles to win many battles, and you can do the same.

Pray this prayer with me.

Father, in the Name of Jesus, I believe even more now that Jesus came to give me a life of abundance, a life of victory in every area, a life of the blessing overflowing in every part of my life, and I receive it right now. I repent for doubting You and Your Word. I repent for speaking my words about the situation instead of Yours, but today, I change and commit to seeing things Your way. I commit to doing things Your way. Father, forgive me for giving up and handing over to the enemy those dreams and desires You placed in my heart. Again, I will pick up those dreams and aspirations and water them with prayer, praise, and the Word of God and see You bring the fulfillment. Devil, in the Name of Jesus, I recognize you as the thief, and I bind and rebuke you in Jesus' Name, and I command every demonic assignment, plan, and work to be null, void and destroyed.

Father, thank You that it is not by any works I do or not do that will secure my promised land, but putting my faith in Jesus who already purchased everything I will ever need. I say I believe I have received His victory being manifested, dreams, and desires being fulfilled now in every area of my life. In Jesus' Name…Amen.

CHAPTER 2
I Had No Idea

By Karen Hawkins

I Had No Idea

By Karen Hawkins

As for you, what you intended against me for evil, God intended for good, in order to accomplish a day like this - to preserve the lives of many people.

Genesis 50:20 (Berean)

I was sitting at my kitchen table one morning listening to the song Holy is the Lord, and I don't know what brought up the memory about when I was married living in Altus, Oklahoma. I began to think about the day the Lord saved me from committing suicide, and what brought me to that point. I was going down a road with the thought of driving my car off the edge to get my world, which had fallen apart to stop because I could think of no other way out.

I began to remember all the things I had done to destroy my marriage. You see, I am not one of those women who can look back and say I was a good girl. I could probably say I was one of those good girls until I was about 18 and heartbroken. After that point, I set out on a path of destruction because I felt as if there was no good in me so why not live as I wanted, get what I wanted and do whatever I wanted with whomever I wanted.

When I married at the age of 26, I married out of fear of being along and losing a good man, but I had NO IDEA what marriage was all about or the commitment it commanded. We had lived together for a few years, and

31

since he was going into the service, we got married so I could go with him. Afterward, I lived my life married but single. I lived as if I had the freedom to come and go and do as I pleased without any consideration of the ramifications that came along with it. Then one day, three years later riding down the road on my way to the club, I realized everything I ever thought I wanted I already had. So, I turned my car around and headed home. What I did not know at the time was that it was a little too late. The thankful and dutiful wife I now desired to be now had a husband who no longer wanted me.

Brokenhearted once again. My husband left our home and started living the life as I once did except his life was out in the open, and the person he was with wanted me to know it. Then one Sunday morning there was one too many straws put on my back, and I broke. I found myself riding down this road. It had three wooden bridges you had to cross, and each plank on each bridge made a distinct thumping sound as you went across. I passed one bridge crying out to the Lord for help because I had enough, and I couldn't take anymore. I crossed the second bridge, and I cried out Lord stop the world I want to get off. I looked at the speedometer which indicated I was traveling about 94 mph. Still crying out, I heard the Lord say Karen suicide is one thing I cannot forgive. I closed my eyes because the next stop was the third bridge and then the end.

Except when I opened my eyes, I found myself sitting at the traffic light one block from my house. I have no Idea how I got there. How did my car get turned around? How did I get to a place that was in the opposite direction from where I was headed and stopped at that traffic light? How? I went on to the house. I knew I had to leave that place, that town, that day, but I had no money and no way to get out. However, I still felt that if I didn't leave that place, my life would come to an end.

Everything about me broke that day, and it was far from graceful as we would think it to be. Today looking back, I would have to say the grace of God had worked overtime that day in my life. When I returned to my house that day, I called home to my parents and told them I wanted to come home right then. They had never heard me distraught as I was that day, but I thank God for a praying mother, and although I don't remember hearing my father pray except over meals, I believe even he went before the Lord on my behalf. God sent someone to my house that day to rescue and watch over me until I could get my affairs in order and leave properly. That day I was ready to abandon everything, my job, and everything I owned to get away.

I left for Alabama, and my husband went to Korea. Not much changed in my life. I pushed all those things down into my garbage can of life and defaulted back to my old way of living even though, in the back of my mind, I had hoped for some reconciliation between us. However, that did not happen, he came home mid-tour, and whatever hope I had was ripped to shreds, and I found myself heartbroken again. I moved out of the house I was in and moved back in with my parents. I needed help to get myself on track. Shortly after I moved back in, I received divorce papers in the mail.

I remember passing my mother in the hallway one day, and she handed me this pocket English version bible with all these yellow stickies in it. She said to me there are many things your father and I can fix, but this is one thing only God can do. I locked up in my room for three days reading and re-reading every passage she had marked out and then some. I prayed and prayed to ask God to forgive me for all I had done and for the shameful way I had lived my life. I wrote my husband a letter that was the size of a mini book. I poured out all the good, the bad, the ugly, and why, and I asked him to forgive me. When I emerged from that room, God had lifted the weight and burden of my marriage from my shoulders, and I knew I would be okay.

I had no idea what was up ahead for me, but for the first time in a long while, I could breathe. I don't know if I will ever be able to tell the whole story of what happened during those three years, but what I can say is this, the God I have come to know, and love will allow things to occur in our life that will break us. How that happens and the effects it brings is determined by our reaction to the things that come up in our lives. My life did not have to take the course it took, but the decisions, choices I made determined the roads I would take, and on those roads were all the lumps and bumps I went through. On those roads, some exits led to a better path to better choices with much better outcomes. I just chose to ignore the exits and kept on going. It was another three years after my mother handed me that Bible that I sat in my bed three o'clock in the morning once again crying out to the Lord to take control of my life declaring I was out of control and the more I tried to fix me, the worse I got. God did what I asked Him to do. That was January 17, 1985. I will not lie and say after that night everything was hunky-dory, but I had taken the exit that led me to the cross of Christ, and from a place, I never want to go back.

I've shared this story because as I was sitting at the breakfast table and began to think about all of this, I realized that God does gracefully break us. The Lord took me through stages in my life, removing or cutting things from my life as if He was picking peddles off a rose blossom. One thing at a time, step by step. I began to see looking at my life that If God were to remove all those things at one time the trauma at least for me, would have been astronomical and I would not have been able to bear it.

I had no idea there were choices and consequences for the decisions I made that the enemy of my life meant to use for my destruction, yet at each turn, God changed it for my good because God had another plan. Every time God worked those things out, each one put me on a different road, which eventually leads directly to him.

Genesis 50:20 (Berean) - As for you, what you intended against me for evil, God intended for good, in order to accomplish a day like this - to preserve the lives of many people.

What was happening in Genesis 50 - Joseph's father had died. After Joseph buried his father, his brothers were afraid Joseph might take this opportunity to exact revenge against them for the things they had done to him. They sent a message to Joseph supposedly from their father, asking Joseph to forgive his brothers for what they had done. Joseph replied to them don't be afraid, what you intended for evil God has turned for good. Joseph had no idea that the things his brother had done, and all the things he had to suffer through would bring them to the place of provision.

What I saw in this scripture was at every turn I made, every decision I made, and those decisions others made against me, every time, in the end, God turned it for my good to bring me to this place and to accomplish His design and desire for my life. Now I feel as though I need to make some clarifications, so no one gets things twisted. God did not put the experiences I had on me or in my life. God allows us to choose which way we want to go, and if we choose something other than His way, He will let us go through the consequences of our choices. In the book of James, the scripture tells us that we are drawn away by our lusts and desires, which gives birth to sin; God does not tempt us with evil. He will extend His grace and mercy towards us as we repent and turn to him. As we do this, it will allow God to change our bad decisions and possibly lessen the consequences to work out for our benefit and useable to change or have a positive effect on the lives of those around us. There are instances where God will intervene on our behalf as He did for me that day in Oklahoma. It was God who turned my car around and put it in the direction of my home. However, that type of intervention happened only one other time in my life as far as I can recall. 2 Chronicles 7:14 tells us that if we (God's people) will humble ourselves, pray and seek His face and turn from our wicked (twisted) ways THEN, He will hear from heaven and will heal our land (intervene on our behalf). That day in Oklahoma I had gotten as low as I could get and all I could think of was to cry out to the Lord for help, and He heard me and started the healing process by saving my life.

Being gracefully broken, God does not expose our dirty laundry when He breaks us. God comes alongside us to strengthen and comfort us. As we allow God's spirit and influence to take place where our spirit and worldly influence used to reign, we become weakened in our strength and stronger in HIM! The enemy would have us broken, and our guts spilled out in the streets for all to see, but I thank God for His grace and mercy towards us.

Three years after the events that took place in Oklahoma, I found myself sitting in the middle of my bed at 3 a.m., once again, crying out to the Lord. Except for this time, I was not asking God to get me out of a troublesome situation. I was asking Him to take control of my life because I realized the more I tried to fix me, the worse I became. I had no idea what the ramifications of my request would be I only knew something in my life had to change. Only this time, I was willing to surrender.

When God steps into your life, things begin to change. For me, it was though I had gotten on a train that was swiftly going down the track. The thing about that was I didn't want to get off. Amazing things started to occur. I did not tell anyone what I had asked the Lord to do for me, but my friends began to see the change before I did and suddenly, they gradually faded away along with my desire for my old way of living.

Within a few months, I moved into a new house with my name on it. Leading up to this, I had been in a relationship for a few years, and even though my heart was attached, inside, I knew it was wrong. I began to ask the Lord if this relationship was not what He has for me, take it away. At work, I started attending a noonday bible study. One afternoon we talked about having the strength to overcome. I realized I had been praying wrong, which is why I had not gotten an answer from God. So, I began to pray Lord if this is not what You have for me, give me the strength to overcome because I didn't have the strength to say no. I didn't want to move into my new house with that hanging over me, but shortly after I moved in, one night something rose up on the inside of me and I declared no more. That night was the end, and I started a brand-new life. After that, a hunger stirred within me to find out about this God and the love He had for me because it was something I had never experienced before. I had no idea the joy and peace that came along with living in Christ. I remember the night I asked God to take control of my life. I told God the only thing I wanted was to repair my relationship with my father and for peace of mind. I thank God because He gave me both. Don't get me wrong, life has not been a bed of roses, but I would not trade the life Christ gave me with anything the world has to offer.

You may wonder why I wrote this chapter and shared some of my stories? I'm glad you asked. Before I committed my life to Christ, I had a friend named Rosalind. Rosalind would always talk about "MY JESUS" as if He was personal and only belonged to her. Every time she would say "MY JESUS," it piqued my interest. So, I began to read the Bible to find out about "THIS JESUS" because I did not know Him, and I never heard anyone refer to Him so personally. I had no idea that this point in my journey would lead me to that night at 3 a.m. Jesus was so personal to her, and I wanted Him to be personal for me as well. As my relationship with the Lord grew, I began to wonder about the people, friends, and family I had left behind.

Then one day an old friend came by my house to ask me to pray for his girlfriend who was struggling with drug addiction. Later that night, as I was praying for her and others as I had done many times before, I began to ask the Lord what about all the people I had left behind. What about them. I said, "Lord, I am tired of watching the devil eat their lunch, and I have the answer, and that answer is Jesus. Lord, You did it for me, why not them?" The Lord asked me to count the cost for what I was asking. Once again, I had NO IDEA what I was asking. All I knew was there were people I knew, friends and family, who were suffering through life with addictions and an array of problems, and I had the answer. The Lord said to count the cost. My only reply to Him was how could I say no.

So, what began to happen. People would come to me at work and church, people I didn't know. Strangers would start to tell me their life stories or talk about the issues they were having with their wife, their children, and so forth. I would sit there in amazement wondering why these people are talking to me and what in the world was I supposed to tell them when they finished. Every time, God would give me the words to say and to pray. I had no clue, no idea where all of this was going but I was on for the ride.

I would study and share what God had shared with me. Sometimes He had just shared it the night before, and I loved it. I wanted to see the change in others that God had made in me. The purpose of this chapter and this book is to share what the Lord has done in and through our lives to let others know there is hope; there is a God that will love as no one else can.

Jeremiah 29:11 – "For I know the plans I have for you," says the Lord. "They are plans for good and not for disaster, to give you a future and a hope."

I cannot begin to share the numerous things the Lord has done in my life. He has wrapped His arms around me in some of my darkest moments. Jesus has protected me from things I did not see. The Lord has provided for me far beyond anything I could have imagined. He gave me hope when I had none or when I could not see my way. God has been so good to me even when it appeared, I was determined to bump my head. God is who He says He is, and God will do what He says He will do whether we have any idea what that may be. I had no idea that my life could turn out as it has, but then I'm not the orchestrator of my life and having "NO IDEA" was the best thing for me.

My prayer for You:

Father, I thank You for being such a loving and caring God and for choosing us to be Your sons and Your daughters. Lord, I thank You for making way for us even in our darkest moments. Lord, I pray for each person reading these pages that something was said that will draw them closer to You. Lord I pray and thank You for being no respecter of persons and what You did for me You will do for all who are will. Lord, heal the hurts and mend the wounds. Help repair broken relationships because Lord there is nothing too hard for You to do. Forgive us for the things we have done, whether it was a thought, a word or a deed and set our feet on the path that will always lead to You. Give hope to those who feel there is no hope. Turn lives around just as You turned that car and my life around. Help us to fix our eyes forward on You and not on the things in our past. Thank You, Lord, for not only hearing our prayer but for answering them in Jesus name, Amen!

CHAPTER 3

Broken Hallelujah

By Sharon Kornegay

Broken Hallelujah

By Sharon Kornegay

Praise the LORD! Praise the LORD, O my soul! 2 I will
praise the LORD while I live; I will sing praises to my
God while I have my being
Psalm 146:1-2 (NASB)

To utter the word "Hallelujah" is to express worship and
praise to God. It is translated to mean, "God be praised!"
"Praise ye the Lord" is also used. The first part of the
word, "hallelu" instructs hearers to praise. The last syllable,
"jah," is considered a shortened form of the name of God,
who is often referred to as Lord, Yahweh, and Jehovah.
The Greek form of the word "Alleluia" means the very
same thing. Hallelujah appears several times in the Bible.
In many instances, it appears in the Old Testament at the
opening or closing of a Psalm. In the New Testament, the
term appears exclusively in Revelation 19.

What happens when your Hallelujah is broken? Perhaps
the music has stopped, you have left the church and can
no longer dance. Maybe life has hit you hard, and you feel
all alone and broken. If you are like me, you may have
called on your friends, and no one was available to talk to
you. I have felt the kind of pain and heartache that you
may be experiencing. I know what it is like to be going
through a tough time. I have cried many times over wrong
decisions and connections with people who were
deceptive and mean-spirited. I have been in the place

where I felt trapped with nowhere to go. Many times, I asked God to deliver me. My Hallelujah was broken. I knew I was supposed to lift my hands in worship, but I could not. I wanted to be free from the heartache but did not know how to be free. I prayed over and over again for answers, but none came. So, what did I do? After I finished crying and pouting, I had to come to the realization that although my heart was hurting, God knew about it. Therefore, I had to learn to trust God with my disappointment and whatever issue I was facing that was causing me to feel sorrowful.

Many times, we refuse to honestly confront brokenness. It is much easier to take a non-direct approach rather than admit our shortcomings. However, when we do not assess where we are and how we got there, we will end up feeling lost and broken. Hopelessness will become the front seat driver. It is a hard feeling to be crying at home and also shedding tears of sorrow at church. Yet, we walk about in a robotic state and pretend that everything is fine while leading others around us to believe that we are shedding tears of joy. On the other hand, there are instances where those close to us may know that we are hurting but don't know what they can do to help. Some may even misuse scripture and make you feel worse than you are already feeling.

When sorrow enters a person's heart, it must be dealt with. I read an article written by the Mayo Clinic staff members and was surprised to learn of the "Broken Heart Syndrome." Broken Heart Syndrome (BHS) is a temporary heart condition that's often brought on by stressful situations (mayoclinic.org). I wonder how many saints are suffering from BHS. One of the most common and distressing afflictions of the human race is depression. While it is true that even as Christians, we struggle with our emotions, it is unlikely that you will find the word depression in the Bible, (except in the New Living Translation and maybe some of the newer versions that I have yet to read). The Bible uses words such as downcast, sad, forlorn, discouraged, downhearted, mourning, troubled, miserable, despairing, and brokenhearted. The scriptures provoke us to praise the Lord. Now, I know that typically, it is easy to get involved in the external aerobics of praise and worship. But God is looking for the true worshippers who will worship Him in both Spirit and in truth. We were created to give God glory (Ref: Psalm 24:1, Psalm 89:11, and Psalm 98:8). In reality, some people do not have the strength to constantly battle in the spiritual realm. Spiritual warfare is exhausting, especially if you do not have others standing alongside you to help. Whether we admit it or not, there are people we know who are right now asking God to free them from the chains that have them bound. Others have given up and thrown in the towel. Some may be contemplating suicide, even though they are a Christian. Many people in the Bible exhibited symptoms of what I describe as the broken hallelujah syndrome: Hagar, Moses, Naomi, Hannah, Saul, David, Solomon, Elijah, Nehemiah, Job, Jeremiah, John the Baptist, Judas Iscariot, Paul, and Jesus… just to name a few. We must pray and ask God to help us discern the true depths of the contents of the heart. Through spiritual encroachment, Satan invades the hearts of people. He takes a stealth approach, and deposits fear doubt and unbelief. Encroachment is sometimes resolved with a simple conversation with someone, but at other times, the issues must be taken to God in prayer. The enemy enjoys attacking our emotions. But our emotions do not authenticate truth. Rather, our emotions authenticate our understanding of the truth. Psalms 146:5-8 (NASB):

> 5How blessed is he whose help is the God of Jacob, Whose hope is in the LORD his God, 6Who made heaven and earth, The sea and all that is in them; Who keeps faith forever; 7Who executes justice for the oppressed; Who gives food to the hungry. The LORD sets the prisoners free. 8The LORD opens the eyes of the blind; The LORD raises up those who are bowed down; The LORD loves the righteous.

My prayer is that the truth of the Word of God will begin to strike our lives with the power and forcefulness of the Holy Spirit and set us free. The Holy Spirit has a significant and fundamental role in our emotions. We cannot touch God without our emotions being involved. Even when God touches us, our emotions are still involved. He is the one who gave us tears, joy, laughter, and even anger. Our emotions partner with both the joys and tragedies of life. As triune beings, we possess a spirit, soul, and body. If you are suffering from a broken hallelujah, you must begin to ask the Spirit of God to address your inner life. The Holy Spirit's experience within us is deeply emotional. It is one thing to acknowledge Jesus as the Son of God from afar, but God wants intimacy. He wants us to acknowledge Him daily. If you have accepted Jesus Christ as Lord and Savior of your life, then you can confidently embrace His love. The indwelling of the Holy Spirit governs our lives and provides us with the opportunity to truly worship Him. Psalm 28 (NASB) The LORD is my strength and my shield; My heart trusts in Him, and I am helped; Therefore, my heart exults, And with my song, I shall thank Him. God wants to help us. Let's read some examples of emotional distress. Matthew 26:6-13 (NASB):

> Now when Jesus was in Bethany, at the home of Simon, the leper, [7]a woman came to Him with an alabaster vial of very costly perfume, and she poured it on His head as He reclined at the table. [8]But the disciples were indignant when they saw this, and said, "Why this waste? [9]"For this perfume might have been sold for a high price and the money given to the poor." [10]But Jesus, aware of this, said to them, "Why do you bother the woman? For she has done a good deed to Me. [11]"For you always have the poor with you; but you do not always have Me. [12]"For when she poured this perfume on My body, she did it to prepare Me for burial. [13]"Truly I say to you, wherever this gospel is preached in the whole world, what this woman has done will also be spoken of in memory of her.

The Bible says, "They were indignant." They acted out of character because the woman used costly oil to anoint Jesus' feet. They responded out of their emotions. In actuality, they revealed their brokenness. How did Jesus react to their indignation? He responded with the truth. He did not allow the woman to be moved by their indignation. He was touched by her action. He opposed those who were opposing her. He declared that what she did would be spoken of in her memory throughout the world, wherever the Gospel was preached.

Let us look at how Jesus handled His own negative emotions in Matthew 26:36-45 (NASB):

> [36]Then Jesus came with them to a place called Gethsemane, and said to His disciples, "Sit here while I go over there and pray." [37]And He took with Him Peter and the two sons of Zebedee and began to be grieved and distressed. [38]Then He *said to them, "My soul is deeply grieved, to the point of death; remain here and keep watch with Me."
>
> [39]And He went a little beyond them, and fell on His face and prayed, saying, "My Father, if it is possible, let this cup pass from Me; yet not as I will, but as You will. "[40]And He came to the disciples and found them sleeping, and said to Peter, "So, you men could not keep watch with Me for one hour? [41]Keep watching and praying that you may not enter into temptation; the spirit is willing, but the flesh is weak."
>
> [42] He went away again a second time and prayed, saying, "My Father, if this cannot pass away unless I drink it, Your will be done." [43]Again He came

and found them sleeping, for their eyes were heavy. [44]And He left them again, and went away and prayed a third time, saying the same thing once more. [45]Then He *came to the disciples and said to them, "Are you still sleeping and resting? Behold, the hour is at hand, and the Son of Man is being betrayed into the hands of sinners.

Jesus fulfilled the will of God. Despite what He saw and felt, He did not allow His emotions to get the best of Him. He dealt with His brokenness through prayer. He bowed on His face and worshipped God. He had to choose to truthfully confront where He was emotionally and ask God to give Him strength. He told God, "Let this cup pass from me, but if You do not, Your will be done."

Praise and worship still the hand of the enemy. God deserves true worship. Worship heals and transforms our minds. Worship takes us where we cannot go on our own through fleshly promptings. Worship pleases God. If we refuse to worship, especially when we have a broken hallelujah, we will remain defeated. Satan hates to see our worship because worship causes us to reflect on and appreciate the majesty of Almighty God. True worship extends beyond a mere slow song. True worship demands God's attention. The scriptures provide us with many examples of how to react when situations cause us to have a broken hallelujah. Jesus kept God first in all things. He wanted us to know that if depression should ever try to firmly grip our lives, Satan is behind it. However, Satan does not stand a chance of winning against God. God has given us the victory through the Blood of His Son, Jesus

Christ. Things will get better for you so don't give up. God knows how to heal what is broken. Therefore, stand strong and oppose the one who is opposing you. Open up your Bible, read the scriptures, and begin to worship the Father in Spirit and in truth. You will pass the test. Even though your hallelujah may be broken, weeping endures for a night, but joy will come to you, in the morning.

My Prayer For You:

Heavenly Father, let this mind be in me that was also in Christ Jesus. When my heart is overwhelmed, lead me to the Rock that is higher than I am. Thank You for the precious Blood of Jesus Christ that was shed for me. He gave me deliverance, peace, victory, and salvation. I thank You for renewing my mind by Your Word and for transforming my thoughts so that they do not conform to the patterns of this world. Father, through the Blood of Jesus Christ, I triumph over depression and every wicked power of the enemy that is meant to destroy me. I rebuke and bind all activities of Satan that have been launched against me. Father, I trust You and humbly embrace Your plan for my life. Thank You for healing my heart. In Jesus name, I pray, Amen.

CHAPTER 4
Broken and Victorious

By Karen Hawkins

Broken and Victorious

By Karen Hawkins

What do you think of when you think of being broken?

In May 2018, I was diagnosed with breast cancer. I remember the day I received the call from the radiologist. She said my test results did not come back with the diagnosis we had hoped for, and I realized at that moment, I had to choose between faith or fear. I also realized this was one of those moments for which Jesus died. The thing that amazes me about that time is I don't recall feeling much of anything which also surprises me considering my family history with cancer. My father, my mother, my maternal grandmother and my sister all diagnosed with different forms of cancer and only one out of four of them had what we would call a success rate; yet they all succeeded because the Bible says absent from the body, present with the Lord.

As I began to walk through the process of all the examinations, treatment options and so on, I did not think that I had already been set up by God to overcome the fear that usually comes along with the diagnosis of cancer. Going through the treatment process, I had such a great peace within me. I'm not a dramatic type of person, but things do tend to bother me when I cannot figure them out or see my way through to the other side. In this case, I could not figure it out nor know how the end or how the other side would look. However, there were decisions I had to make, and the only thing I could rely on was the peace God had given me. Isaiah 26:3 (AMP) says "You will keep in perfect and constant peace the one whose mind is steadfast [that is, committed and focused on You - in both inclination and character]. Because he trusts and takes refuge in You [with hope and confident expectation]."

There are not many things that bring life into focus like the pronouncement of cancer. God said in Jeremiah 29:11 that He has plans for us, and these plans are to prosper us and to give us hope AND a future, all the things cancer is not designed to do. Thinking back, I remember one Sunday morning the praise team sang a song that said let all the other names fade away, and Jesus take Your place, and I began to think about how the Bible says the name of Jesus is above every name, this means even the name cancer.

During this time the Lord gave me flashbacks of things I had learned, things others have said, things written in the Word of God and things I had taught over the years concerning healing and God's plan, God's place in and for our lives. It was now time for me to come to terms with what I truly believed. Are God and the Word of God real in "MY" life? Am "I" indeed a child of God and heir to the promises of God or not? In this process, I was broken and yet victorious all at the same time.

When we think of the word broken, most of the time it is in terms of something destroyed, ruined and no longer useable. I had a glass pitcher someone gave me as a wedding present some years ago, and I broke it and had to throw it out because it was no longer useable. There are things, habits, thoughts, and actions that need to be destroyed and made no longer useable in our lives. However, there is a brokenness that comes from the Lord that allows the unusable things in our lives to be removed without destroying us so that when He is finished, what is left feels, walks and talks more like Him!

During the process, there were times when I had both types of brokenness in operation. I had brokenness where there were things in my life that needed to be destroyed and removed and also brokenness that would allow God to show himself faithful and make me more like Him. Being broken even by God does not always feel good. I wasn't jumping up and down shouting Hallelujah. There were parts of my life that appeared shattered, and at times, I felt old and useless. There were things I thought I had that were strengths which turned out to be nothing more than pride by another name. Those things were broken and removed, leaving me feeling fragile, and the thought of being fragile scared me, but something a friend told me years ago came to mind. He said, "Karen, you don't like feeling vulnerable," and he was right. To me, being fragile or vulnerable meant something or someone would have the ability to hurt me, so in my mind, I needed to feel in control. Have you ever been in a situation where you felt as though things are happening to or around you and you could not change or stop it, and all you can do is go along for the ride? That is how I felt.

Those are the times when you want to step back and ask God "really" or say, "you have got to be kidding." It is also in those moments, the strength and power of God begin to rise to the surface, and you know that you are not alone. It is the power and love of God at work in you that carries and brings you through to the other side.

Gracefully broken. Grace meaning the spirit and influence of God operating in us to regenerate and strengthen us. When you add the ending "fully" to the word grace, it forms an adverb meaning to be wholly, absolutely, thoroughly and altogether filled with the spirit and influence of God. John 3:30 says God must increase or become greater in us, and we must decrease or become less. Gracefully broken and victorious. As we allow God to increase in us, His grace – His spirit and influence, begin to take the place where our spirit and worldly influence used to work and reign in our lives. There is something special, uncanny, or beyond the ordinary that takes place within us when we are broken in the Lord. When we give our lives to the Lord, and we allow God to start working in us, we become broken – weakened in our strength while becoming stronger in the Lord and the power of His might and not our own. When the spirit and power of God influence us, it may appear as though we have changed directions abruptly, but as we allow God to work, there is an anointing given that enables us to change. We must remember God said He has plans for us, and when we begin to follow His plan and direction, what was once broken will start to reveal our victory in Jesus.

Praise be to the God and Father of our Lord Jesus Christ. God is the Father, who is full of mercy and all comfort. He comforts us every time we have trouble, so when others have trouble, we can comfort them with the same comfort God gives us.

2 Corinthians 1:3-4 (NCV)

Throughout scripture, we have examples of people gracefully broken so that when we find ourselves in that place, and every one of us will be there at some point in our life, we will know that God can lift us victorious. Let's look at Moses for an example. Moses was raised in Pharaoh's house as a son but born a Hebrew. Moses thought that because of his privilege in Pharaoh's house; he could come to the rescue and defend one of his people, a Hebrew in a fight. Moses killed the Egyptian and hid the body. The next day, he attempted to come to the rescue again, this time the fight was between two Hebrews. However, this time, Moses was rejected by his own people then cast out by Pharaoh for what he had done the day before. Moses went from the palace to a place of exile, from a son at Pharaoh's table to a servants table in Midian with a price on his head. Moses was broken to get the pride of Pharaoh's house out of him, which later enabled him to come to the place of dependency on God.

David is another example. He was anointed to be king at a young age. He enjoyed success in the fields, success over the Philistines, and victory in war as a soldier. David became king with the power and pride to do whatever his heart desired. The Bible says pride comes before a fall, and his pride and power led him to desire and possess something that was not his to have – another man's wife. The book of James says we are drawn away by our own

59

lust and desire giving birth to sin, which if allowed to grow ends up in death.

In this case, the death that occurred was not that of David but Uriah Bathsheba's husband. David was drawn away by his desire for this beautiful woman, and through that desire, they conceived a son. In his ambition to conceal his adultery, David ordered Uriah put in a place that would ensure his death but what he did not know was it also eventually ensured the death of his Son. We must remember that the things we do and say don't always affect us directly but can influence other people in our lives.

David was broken not by what he had done. David's breaking came from the Word of the Lord given through the Prophet Nathan, which afterward, David said to Nathan, "I have sinned against the Lord." And Nathan said to David, "The Lord also has put away your sin; you shall not die. Nevertheless, because by this deed you have utterly scorned the Lord, the child who is born to you shall die." 2 Samuel 12:13-14 (ESV)

The next example is Peter, a disciple of Jesus. Peter was a successful fisherman by trade and walked with the Lord for three years. He sat at Jesus' feet, ate at His table, and was taught firsthand by the Son of the living God. Peter witnessed many miracles and was bold enough to draw his sword in defense of his master Jesus; yet when the time came for him to stand up and be accountable for what and in whom he said he believed, Peter broke down, denied Jesus and ran away in fear and shame.

Three men, each realized they were broken by what was inside them, pride, lust, and fear. However, this was not the end of their stories. The scripture in Micah 7:7-8 (NLT) says, "As for me, I look to the Lord for help. I wait confidently for God to save me, and my God will certainly hear me. Do not gloat over me, my enemies! For though I fall, I will rise again. Though I sit in darkness, the Lord will be my light."

In this passage, verse 8 says do not Gloat or Rejoice over me my enemy (pride, lust, and fear), for when I fall (when I am broken) I shall rise again (I will rise victorious). When I sit in darkness (in my brokenness), the Lord will be my light (He will show me the way).

Verse 7 – I will look to the Lord, I will wait for the God of my salvation, and my God will hear me. The purpose of being gracefully broken yet victorious is to convey that even though things happen in our lives that seem to be against everything we want or believe, when all hell breaks loose against us, when our spirits are down and challenged, you don't give up, you don't give in, and you don't give out. The God of our salvation will cause us to rise no matter what the outcome "IF" we will continue to stand firm in him. God's will be done because He said He has plans for us that are good and not evil to give us hope and a future and in that we win.

The scripture says in 2 Corinthians 1:3-4 God, the Father is full of mercy (He does not give us what we rightly deserve.) He comforts us (encourages, provides help, and stands alongside) every time we have trouble. He does this so when others have trouble we can comfort (encourage, provide help, and stand alongside) them with the same comfort God gave us.

Jesus, our best example was broken in the Garden of Gethsemane when he said Father if there be any other way, take this cup from me. Jesus knew the road ahead of Him would not be easy but full of pain, yet he rose victorious when he said not my will, but Your will be done. So now if Jesus had to go through, we cannot be surprised when our time of brokenness presents itself. God's purpose or intent for us going through a season of brokenness is not to cause us to hurt but to create a change in us so that through us we can show His love and compassion to someone else. Remember the scripture in 2 Corinthians says so we can comfort them with the same comfort God gave us.

When I received the diagnosis and began the treatment process, I had such a peace that it almost bothered me to the point I was wondering if there was something wrong. In prayer one day the Lord said I had peace because it was in me and He began to show me how I had been praying the prayer of faith for healing every day for years on the prayer line. God also gave me a living example of the scripture in 2 Corinthians in Minister Meghan Prude because she went through the same process and without asking she came alongside me, encouraged me, gave help and stood by my side when they stuck me with the needles and hooked me up to all those drugs. She walked me through the process before it began so I would know what to expect and even when to expect it while letting me know all I had to do was hold on because the light switch will be flipped, and this too shall pass. One of my concerns during this time was my family's reaction. My daughter after I told her what was going on, asked me what God said and after I told her what the Lord said to me, she simply said well that's what we will stand on. The God of my salvation heard me and lifted me up victorious.

The comfort God gave Minister Meghan, she gave to me, and I had the opportunity to give it to another woman as she started her process. That day she sat there broken, but God lifted her up. One thing God was trying to get me to see in all of this, is this life is not about me, it is all about Jesus – why because He lived and died for me, for Meghan and all of you! It's not about us; it's all about HIM! Also, because of that, we have an enemy who comes in many forms, but bottom line his focus and sole purpose are to steal, kill and destroy any hope, comfort or assurance we have in Christ. That enemy whether its cancer, leukemia, diabetes, kidney failure, our children are going astray, a spouse acting up, finances or job loss, the enemy comes for one purpose which is to separate us from the plan, purpose, power, and promise of God for our lives.

God's plan and purpose for Moses were to set His people free to fulfill His promise to bring them to the dwelling place that flowed with milk and honey. God's plan and purpose for David were to have someone in his lineage sit on the throne of Israel to fulfill His promise, and through his line, Jesus was born. God's plan and purpose for Peter were for him to preach the gospel, the good news that there is forgiveness in Jesus and to be saved, he said repent and be baptized.

Had Moses not been broken, he would have believed it was by his hand and not the power of God that the people of Israel were set free. David would have thought because he was king, he could do and take whatever he wanted, and there would be no consequences or price to pay. Peter would have believed he was too weak; his shame was too much, and there was no hope for him, so his only choice was to default and returned to fishing.

Three men, broken by pride, lust, and fear, but as I said earlier, that was not the end of their story. Moses didn't give up the urge to be a deliverer because it was still there when he went to Midian and helped protect Jethro's daughters. David didn't give up after the Prophet Nathan called him out for his sin. His desire to be a man after God's heart led him to repent before the Lord as recorded in Psalm 51 where he wrote

1Have mercy upon me, O God, According to Your lovingkindness; According to the multitude of Your tender mercies, Blot out my transgressions. 2Wash me thoroughly from my iniquity and cleanse me from my sin. 3For I acknowledge my transgressions, and my sin is always before me. 4Against You, You only, have I sinned, and done this evil in Your sight - That You may be found just when You speak, and blameless when You judge

Psalm 51:1-4 (NKJV)

David knew, and we must realize when we sin it is against God and God alone, which is why confession and repentance are so important.

Peter gave in and ran when he realized he had done exactly what Jesus said he would do, but Peter did not give up because he answered the call when Jesus asked, "Peter do you love me?" On the day of Pentecost, Peter was the first disciple to stand up and preach the gospel to those who stood by, and the men asked what must I do to be saved?

When the doctors diagnosed me with breast cancer, one thing I remember hearing was my pastor's voice when he was told about his daughter's diagnosis; he said he had to have a word from the Lord. I turned my face to God and said Lord, I need to hear from YOU! I began to cry out to the Lord, and God began to speak. The Lord told me that this was only a distraction. I would live and not die and would declare the glory of the Lord in the land of the living.

However, let me step back for a moment because there is a significant factor in all of this, I need to point out. It is one thing to be broken, but there is a crucial element that is necessary to come out of brokenness victorious, and that is a relationship with the Lord.

These three men, Moses, David and Peter, each of them if you read their story, you will discover each of them at different points in their lives must have developed a relationship with the Lord. They knew the voice of God and had experienced the power of God working on their behalf.

While there is nothing written regarding Moses' relationship with the Lord before he fled Egypt, Moses was birthed, nursed and raised by his Hebrew mother who taught him the ways and traditions of the Hebrew faith while he enjoyed living as an Egyptian. Something happened between the time he was kicked out of the palace and reached the place in Midian. A humbleness came because when he heard the voice of the Lord, he answered.

David, from a child, knew and enjoyed the presence of the Lord. He learned early on to call upon the name of the Lord for help, strength, and deliverance while tending sheep in his father's field and on the field of battle. Peter was called by Jesus to follow and walk with him. Peter sat at Jesus' feet and was taught firsthand the ways and Word of the Lord. Peter saw the miracles of God come to pass through the Word spoken by Jesus and done by His hand.

From the time Moses was a baby, he was saved and protected because of the prayers of his mother. David, as a young boy, learned how to cry out, worship, and depend on God. Before Jesus was arrested, He told Peter He had prayed for him that his faith would not fail. Then He told Peter when he was converted, to strengthen his brothers. In other words, give them the same comfort, help and stand beside them, just as I have done you.

As for me, many times, I cried out to the Lord, and He delivered and protected me. I had many instances of brokenness in my life. In some of them, I can see where the hand of God was working on my behalf. Other times, I allowed myself to be taken down a very dark path. Like Moses, I thank God for a praying mother and a praying daughter who never gave up on me. I thank God for all those days growing up when my mother made me go to

Sunday School and sit in church. It taught me that when things got too dark for me, I knew whom to call out to and as it is written in Micah chapter 7, the Lord would be my light when I sat in darkness and like Peter, Jesus was my advocate with the Father.

The Bible says the prayers of the righteous avails much. Every one of us at some point in our life will face being broken. It may not be as dramatic as cancer, murder, adultery, or fear. It may just be in our desire to become closer and have a more intimate relationship with God, but regardless of the cause, brokenness still the same.

> James 1:2-4 (MSG) Consider it a sheer gift, friends, when tests and challenges come at you from all sides. You know that under pressure, your faith-life is forced into the open and shows its true colors. So, don't try to get out of anything prematurely. Let it do its work, so you become mature and well-developed, not deficient in any way.

Count it all joy when we are gracefully broken, it will force our faith, what we genuinely believe out into the open and show us our true colors. So, don't give in, don't give up and don't run away. Let it do its work in us, so when that season in our life is finished, we will emerge victoriously. Not only that, we will be able to declare the glory of the Lord and that the devil cannot get what we have.

2 Corinthians 13:5 (AMP) Test and evaluate yourselves to see whether you are in the faith and living your lives as [committed] believers. Examine yourselves [not me]! Or

do you not recognize this about yourselves [by an ongoing experience] that Jesus Christ is in you - unless indeed you fail the test and are rejected as counterfeit?

We are to examine ourselves, take our temperature to see if we are in the faith. Are we hot or cold regarding our relationship with the Lord? This examination is not only, so we will know that God will comfort and help us when we are in trouble. It is so that we will see that He lifts us, carries us through and delivers so that we can comfort those He brings across our paths with the same comfort He has given to us when they go through.

We are gracefully broken - wholly, absolutely, thoroughly and altogether filled with the spirit and influence of God that allows the unusable things in our lives to be removed so that when He is finished what is left feels, walks and talks more like Him! Also, Victorious - so when others have trouble, we can comfort them with the same comfort God gives us. Are you ready?

My prayer for You:

Father God, thank You for giving us another opportunity to lift up the name of Jesus. Lord thank You for coming alongside, strengthening and providing for all that we need in our times of joy and in times of trouble. Lord, I thank You that there is nothing too difficult for You to handle or work out and there is nothing in our lives or on this earth that is greater than You. So, Lord, I pray for all those who are facing physical, mental, or emotional challenges. Lord, we plead and apply the Blood of Jesus over their lives, and we speak healing to their situations. Lord bring the right people across their paths that will lift up their arms and encourage them. Father help each person to see the victory in Christ Jesus regardless of the situation. Help us to share the blessings and deliverance You have given us with those who find themselves in that same place. Lord, we lay the crown of victory at Your feet because it is only You who have and will continue to do these things for us in Jesus name, Amen.

CHAPTER 5
Secretly Broken

By Sharon Kornegay

Secretly Broken

By Sharon Kornegay

Scenario 1: You are an emotional wreck, yet no one understands. Something devastating has occurred in your life. It might have happened in your childhood, in your home or it might be happening right now. It appears to be an unending cycle. You pray and cry. If only you could escape. In a plea of desperation, you ask, "Where are You, Lord? I am longing to hear Your voice." It seems as though you did not hear a response. You feel empty and broken. You are secretly tormented.

Scenario 2: You have got a secret, and your heart hurts. You are deeply wounded. Your pregnancy was the result of a rape. Yep, it happened to you right underneath the stairwell of the church by a ministry leader. Each time you see that person serving among other leaders, you wonder how many other people had a similar experience. Who can you tell or trust? Where do you go? Suddenly, you build up enough courage to openly confess and explain what happened to you. The person you shared your story with appeared to be strong in the Lord. However, they shunned and abandoned you. They turned on you and tarnished your reputation by blaming you for what happened. It was then that you realized how much the enemy hates you and wants you dead!

Scenario 3: You are fighting from within. The Holy Spirit is speaking in one ear, and Satan is speaking in the other one. You have a secret. On the one hand, you are praying, and on the other, you are cussing. Frustration is everywhere. They hate you on the job, at home, and in the church. You have given all of your hard-earned resources for the betterment of the Kingdom of God. You want to be accepted, but the rejection is real. You begin to wonder, "Am I really saved? Does anyone else struggle like me?" The silent treatment and mental abuse are all too real. Your mind is playing tricks on you, and while most of your friends are ministry leaders, they do not say a word. Undoubtfully, they know about your issues, but they turn their heads away from you as if you are a hopeless cause. They always have a Word from the Lord for somebody else but to you, not a word. They look at you as if you are strong when you know you are weak and dying on the inside. It is as if they seem to believe that you want to be where you are, but the reality is you do not know how to escape. You are almost at your breaking point, but the ministry demands are high. They keep asking you to lead worship and keep calling on you to lead the prayer. Your commitment to God is demonstrating an outward yes, but on the inside, you are so broken and empty that it has taken everything you have to keep your head above the water. Warfare is vicious and tormenting. You are afraid; yep, you are extremely scared. When you wake up in the morning, you are gasping for air while your heart races out of control. You continually ask yourself, where can you go? What will you do? How do you survive the daily ambushes of Satan? The only way you can get free is to release your secrets. It is time to tell!

Did the scenarios mentioned above sound familiar? Maybe your testimony is different, but I guarantee something, or someone came to mind when you read them.

After years of serving in ministry, I have learned to recognize the familiar look of hurt in the eyes of broken people. The reason why I can recognize hurt is that for many years, I was hurting but pretended that everything was all right. I knew how to fit in on the church scene even though I was a mess. I would praise God at church only to go home and weep in defeat. There was a secret war going on.

On the one hand, there was worship. On the other, there was warfare. It seemed like there were more times of warfare than of worship. I was being tormented, and the devil was wearing me out. I did not want to trust anybody because everyone that I had previously openly shared my heart with ended up disappointing me. I could not imagine that anyone else in the world was going through like I was going through. Things were hard. I was tired of fighting. I was tired of fighting others and quite frankly was tired of fighting within myself. I decided to talk to God. I had to get to the point where I surrendered totally to His will for my life. I did not want to have anything to do with serving in ministry. I was judging myself wrongly. I rejected me. Others rejected me, and surely I thought God was rejecting me. So, one day, I cried out to Him and asked Him to help me. Even during the times when I could not open my mouth to speak, I would groan and wail from within and ask Him to help me.

I did not only want Him to hear me, but I also wanted Him to answer me quickly. I had to learn many lessons about God. I learned that I could not manipulate Him with my tears. I could not trick Him like I tricked others. He taught me that the manifestation of healing was not going to come through the validation of others. He did not want me to put my confidence and trust in men. Instead, He wanted me to develop a relationship with Him. People saw me but did not see me. They heard me but did not listen to me. I was broken, and no matter how difficult life was for me, I could not adequately describe where I was, and even if I was able to help others realize just how much I hurt, only God could deliver me. God wanted me to accept His love.

There were plenty of times that I walked about numb. I did not know how to articulate what I was going through, and I could not understand how God, who describes Himself as love, would allow me to go through years and years of emotional pain. However, one day, I realized that God never wanted me to depend on my own decisions, nor did He want me to rely on the opinions of my friends. It was an eye-opener when the Holy Spirit reminded me of the choices I made when I disobeyed Him. Although I heard Him instruct me otherwise, I chose to disobey His instructions. He knew in advance that I was getting ready to make detrimental mistakes that would cost me years of pain.

I distinctly remember times when He spoke to me, and I disobeyed. When He spoke to me one day, and it was if I stopped in my tracks. Yes, I remember pausing for a brief moment while the Holy Spirit was speaking. However, I continued to walk towards destruction when all the time I knew deep within that I had just been warned to do otherwise. Prideful disobedience led me down the road to much suffering. Now when I think about it, even if my friends wanted to help me, only God could deliver me. Since I refused to listen to the Holy Spirit, what difference would it have made for me to hear what they had to say? It was time to stop blaming others and making excuses for where I was in life. I finally turned to prayer. I never imagined that my life could be transformed by studying the Word of God and applying its principles to my life. I began accepting the truth of God's love. The circumstances I was encountering kept me on my knees. The more I stayed on my knees, the closer I grew in my relationship with God. He was preparing me to carry the mantle of prayer. He destined for me to minister to a countless number of broken people.

I've had numerous opportunities to share my story. Each time I tell them that transformation happens when we learn to trust in the Lord with all of our hearts and lean not unto our own understanding. I let them know that they are not the only person going through tough times. I tell them about God's love. I inform them to acknowledge Him in all situations, and He will direct them onto the right pathways. Surrendering to God requires repentance. When we repent for doing wrong, we make room for God's Word to come alive in us. His Word illuminates the darkness. It helps us to grow in the grace and knowledge of Who He is. Before surrendering to God, I served Him through words and songs but not actions. Mimicking others resulted in an ungodly mindset which boxed me into a way of thinking that contradicted with His Word. In that ungodly mindset, I thought the lust which I dubbed as being love was comparable to the love of God. However, I later learned the difference between lust and God's unconditional love. My experiences also helped me to learn to love myself. I started reading the Biblical stories about Jesus and started observing biblical patterns. I began realizing that Jesus always ministered to broken people. Although He faced many opportunities to quit, Jesus refused to do so. He stayed focused on fulfilling His God-given assignment on the earth. I wanted the same thing for my life, so I asked God to give me a praying spirit. I heard a voice tell me to open the Bible and begin to talk to God the way David did. I started praying the scriptures. The more I read and prayed, the more I realized that others in the Bible also experienced moments where they were hurt and disappointed. As God continues to deliver me, He is helping me to be bold enough to tell others to obey His voice and not make the same mistakes. He is using me to help others understand they can walk through brokenness with grace.

So, what is grace? Grace means different things to different people. Some have declared that grace is God's unmerited favor. Others have said it is the ability to do what you could not have done on your own without God's help. For me, grace is being still and knowing that He is God. It is the ability to get answers to questions, pass the tests, and soar high like the eagle. Grace is the realization that God has equipped me with His Word while He acts as my enabler. Grace teaches me to rely solely on Him as my keeper. Grace proven confirms to me that He is not only my provider, but He is also my God. Absolutely nothing can happen in my life without God being aware of it. Grace is God's strength, fortified. It is accepting who He is in His fullness. His grace has brought me thus far, and grace will lead me home. His grace is amazing.

Satan spends much time trying to convince us to jump ship. He continually abuses, molests, and rapes people, both spiritually and naturally. However, grace confirms that giving up on God is not an option for His children. We must stand fully clothed in His armor and stubbornly refuse to give the devil the pleasure of destroying our lives. When we stand firm, every one of Satan's darts will fall to the ground even though there may be times when it feels like the hairs on our heads turning grey, God's grace will help us to stand victoriously. God's grace is sufficient. Satan also operates in deception. He places scales over the eyes of people to blind them. He is a liar and consistently paints false images hoping to deter people from following God and turn them onto dark pathways. He blinds people to the truth of God's Word because he realizes that truth sets us free. He loves to isolate and torment us.

God wants us to understand that He has deposited His Spirit in us to help us. He wants us to know that everything we go through is to build our faith. His love is amazing. He captivates us and helps us to stand victoriously against the plans of Satan. He wants our response to be God-centered and Word-driven in every situation. I remind myself over and over again that God cannot lie and whatever He speaks comes to pass. As we prayerfully seek answers from God, our relationship with Him will begin to grow. We have to open up the Bible and pray the Word of God and realize there is a cost for the anointing. We must also recognize that Jesus has already paid the ultimate price for our freedom. His blood sets us free.

Behind the masquerades of pasted smiles are devastated, secretly broken people. Sometimes, people become engrossed in church work as a way to temporarily dismiss what they are encountering both inside and outside of the church. For many, the church is the only outlet they have in which they can freely and safely worship God. For others, the church is just a building because they no longer feel the presence of God.

Even though we may not all be in the same boat and may not experience the oppositional forces of the enemy, we cannot discount, disregard nor minimize the pain that one experiences in their heart when they are hurt. We have all faced challenging situations which lets us know that not everyone has a testimony in which they can declare that all is well. People are sometimes afraid to talk about the challenging things that have happened to them in any - environment, including the church. However, just because they refuse to talk about it, God would still have them to speak up. Revelation 12:11 says we overcome by the blood of the Lamb (Jesus) and the word of our testimony. The church offers a perfect environment to help both victims and abusers to get healed. It is true that select topics are always discussed in church, yet some leaders shy away from the hard and challenging issues that center around sex and perversion. Sometimes, they shy away from tough subjects because they too need deliverance.

Struggles are real. Although our struggles may not be openly discussed, it does not mean that they do not exist, nor will they disappear. Satan takes advantage of challenging situations, and he loves to torment people by inflicting upon them thoughts of defeat. Satan takes pleasure when people isolate themselves from God and others while they mourn secretly. Our minds are not to be the graveyard for secret issues. We must cast our cares upon Jesus because God wants His people free. He does not want us to buy the lies of Satan. As we wait patiently on the Lord for a breakthrough, we must stay in the place of trust in Him. We must know with assurance that He will incline His ear to hear our cries. David said in Psalm 40:1-3 (KJV):

> "I waited patiently for the Lord; and he inclined unto me and heard my cry. [2]He brought me up also out of a horrible pit, out of the miry clay, and set my feet upon a rock, and established my goings. [3]And he hath put a new song in my mouth, even praise unto our God: many shall see it, and fear, and shall trust in the Lord."

We are not defeated. We have to flip the script on the devil and get the same attitude Paul had in Philippians 1:12-26 (NKJV):

"[12]But I want you to know, brethren, that the things which happened to me have actually turned out for the furtherance of the gospel, [13]so that it has become evident to the whole palace guard, and to all the rest, that my chains are in Christ; [14]and most of the brethren in the Lord, having become confident by my chains, are much more bold to speak the word without fear."

[15]Some indeed preach Christ even from envy and strife, and some also from goodwill: [16]The former preach Christ from selfish ambition, not sincerely, supposing to add affliction to my chains; [17]but the latter out of love, knowing that I am appointed for the defense of the gospel. [18]What then? Only that in every way, whether in pretense or in truth, Christ is preached; and in this, I rejoice, yes, and will rejoice.

[19]For I know that this will turn out for my deliverance through your prayer and the supply of the Spirit of Jesus Christ, [20]according to my earnest expectation and hope that in nothing I shall be ashamed, but with all boldness, as always, so now also Christ will be magnified in my body, whether by life or by death. [21]For to me, to live is Christ, and to die is gain. [22]But if I live on in the flesh, this will mean fruit from my labor; yet what I shall choose I cannot tell. [23]For I am hard-pressed between the two, having a desire to depart and be with Christ, which is far better. [24]Nevertheless, to remain in the flesh is more needful for you. [25]And

being confident of this, I know that I shall remain and continue with you all for your progress and joy of faith, [26]that your rejoicing for me may be more abundant in Jesus Christ by my coming to you again."

You are valuable to God. He does not see you as worthless, and He will not sit by idly and allow the enemy to trample you down. In moments when you feel broken, God will help you to walk through it with grace because no one has the right to take advantage of you. God appreciates and honors integrity and truth. Do not ever forget that you are God's precious jewel and He loves You.

My Prayer for You:

Heavenly Father,

Thank You for being God. No matter what I am going through, I thank You for gracing me with the ability to triumph in Christ Jesus. I thank You for purifying my heart and strengthening me through Your Word. I am delivered and made whole, and I trust You with my life. I release every secret thing to You and thank You for taking good care of me. I receive Your love and grace so that I can do all things through Christ Jesus who gives me strength. In Jesus name, I pray, Amen.

CHAPTER 6

Lift Your
Worship Gracefully

By Yolanda Franklin

Lift Your Worship Gracefully

By Yolanda Franklin

Three times I pleaded with the Lord to take it away from me, But He said to me, "My grace is sufficient for you, for my power is made perfect in weakness." Therefore, I will boast all the more gladly about my weaknesses, so that Christ's power may rest on me. 2 Corinthians 12: 8-9 (NIV)

Ten years ago, was the first time I remember crying out to the Lord asking Him to take the pain away. Every day I pursued God, asking Him to change my situation with the assumption that I was in the "throne room" and God being whom He is, had to hear my cry. I was quoting scriptures such as Romans 8:28, "all things work together for the good of them that Love the God, to them who are the called according to His purpose." All the while, convincing myself that I did love God and that I was called to His purpose, not realizing I fell into the "cliché" of religion.

We can convince ourselves of anything at the expense of denying God access to work truth into our life. This process of trying to persuade God to remove my thorn of affliction went on for years then suddenly sitting in the same house ten years later, divorced, broken, hurt, weak, bruised, misunderstood, and in prison to my web of consciousness, GOD SPOKE and said, I am lifting your worship gracefully.

I lifted my eyes and said: "Lord, I thought my life represented You, and my worship was real. So, Lord, what does my worship have to do with You changing my situation and me going through this transition? Why does it hurt? Why do I feel like You are far from me? I feel as if I am giving You my all, but getting anywhere?" God finally said, read 2 Corinthians12:8-9 again, but read it on an empty stomach, in a quiet place, with your eyes focused, and with your mind clear so you can understand the words that I want to feed your spirit. So, I replied, yes Lord, I will.

> 2 Corinthians 12:8-9 (NLT) - Three different times I begged the Lord to take it away. Each time He said, "My grace is all you need. My power works best in weakness. "So now I am glad to boast about my weaknesses so that the power of Christ can work through me.

I read that scripture about 50 times before it finally clicked, and tears began running down my face God reminded me of what it says in Psalm 119:71 (NKJV) "It is good for me that I have been afflicted, that I may learn Your statutes."

Many times, we would like for God to change our circumstance so that we don't have to feel the pain. However, at that moment, God is trying to connect with us in spite of the choices we made, so He allows the pain to come, the hurt to be felt and the disappointment to be manifested, all so we would know the power of Christ to deliver. We cannot see the power without the struggle. It is when we are weak that He is made strong in us. The power and grace of God cannot rest on me for me or all the world to see if He simply removes the thorn.

Then the bombshell came when He said I lifted your worship gracefully. It was God that allowed this transition to take place, and in all the changes, I learned to depend on him. I realized my life was totally in His hands. Despite these and other difficulties, we must believe that our worship, which is our lifestyle to God far outweigh the challenges.

When I have a friend or coworker come to me and say you are glowing, or you are smiling today, or one of my spiritual children say, mommy, you don't look like you have aged at all, that lets me know that I don't look like what I have gone through. After all these years, I realized that worship is not just an opportunity to use musical instruments or singing. It is more than a moment of crying or an emotional state. It is way more than what we do on a Sunday morning. Worship is about what we live for, who and what we love. Worship is about who we are before God. I am a vessel that loves God even with all my issues, and that is precisely what God sees every day. However, when presented to the world, they see a diamond sparkling because of God's grace and mercy, which is fresh and new every day. It provides me the opportunity to shine and continue to excel even amid my thorn-life experiences. So, for me to see God's power resting on me, I had to be made weak.

The Lord Will Use Your Enemy

Have you ever been blindsided by a family member or a friend who at first was so fond of you but then turned on you for no reason at all? Have you been doing what you do best in serving people but then something goes awry and the people you helped shift gears on you? It is never easy to be the bigger person. Oh, how many times have I heard the words, "Do Right No Matter How Someone Treats You." Doing what is right is not always an easy thing to do when you purpose in your heart to do right in the sight of the Lord, and evil is still present. David found himself in this very situation when the Lord decided to use Saul to "Lift Worship Gracefully" within David.

During this time, the Spirit of Jehovah came upon David; and the Spirit of Jehovah departed from Saul. David grew from a child into a hero in war and a scholar in peace. At the same time, Saul declined from being a hero and digressed into a moody and resentful tyrant. Samuel 16:14-23 depicts the story of David and Saul, where David was anointed king at the same time, God rejected Saul as the king of Israel. Saul had an evil spirit that haunted him. He could not control it, and he was advised to hire someone that could play "worship" music to calm his spirit and make him feel better. So, Saul hired David as his Worship Leader. Israel remained under King Saul until God decided the transition was complete.

God allowed David to play the harp to Saul's evil spirit only to prepare him for the next level in his life. Just as

Saul's attitude changed toward David who was there as a servant, others will have a change of heart towards you too; but when your Worship is YES it doesn't matter who is with you, God is your focus. That is the reason David could say he would "touch not thou anointed and do that prophet no harm" because he realized who was in control, and that is God. God was continuing to lift the worship out of David, knowing that he would have to face giants, slay lies, put down ridicule, overcome the enemy and even set his wife's mind free concerning worship

One thing is for sure; worship is not just the songs that the choir sings. Worship is not the money we place in the tithes and offering basket. Worship is not leading a ministry in the church. The Bible says that when we worship, we must worship in spirit and truth. There are various acts or expressions of worship, but they do not always define true worship. There are numerous definitions of the word worship. There is one that encapsulates the priority we should give to worship as a spiritual discipline: Worship is to honor with extravagant love and extreme submission. God wants us to say YES, no matter what and God will get this YES if we love Him sometimes even if He must allow circumstances to happen in our life to lift the worship gracefully. He does not forcefully make us say yes, He enables us to choose. I love how God loves.

True worship is the acknowledgment of God and all His power and glory in everything we do. The highest form of praise and worship is obedience to Him and His Word.

To do this, we must know God; we cannot be ignorant of Him (Acts 17:23). Worship is to glorify and exalt God - to show our loyalty and admiration to our Father. True worship, in other words, is defined by the priority we place on who God is in our lives and where we place God on our list of priorities. True worship is a matter of the heart expressed through a lifestyle of holiness. No matter how David felt betrayed, David demonstrated his love for God. David expressed this by showing the enemy how powerful God is when he revealed to Saul the piece of cloth he took from his garment representing how close he had gotten but spared his life in love.

The apostle Paul described true worship perfectly in Romans 12:1-2 (NASB) "Therefore I urge you, therefore, brethren, by the mercies of God to present your bodies a living and holy sacrifice, acceptable to God which is your spiritual service of worship. And do not be conformed to this world but be transformed by the renewing of your mind so that you may prove what the will of God is, that which is good and acceptable and perfect." Just know that you are exactly where God wants you to be even when it does not feel like it.

A True Heart to Worship

True worship is God-centered. We worship God because He is God Period! Our extravagant love and extreme submission to the Holy One flows out of the reality that God loved us "first." It is highly appropriate to thank God for all the things He has done for us. All too often, we can get caught up in where to worship, what music they should sing in worship, and how worship looks to other people. Focusing on these things misses the point. Worship is a lifestyle and a lifetime commitment, meaning we worship from the heart and the way God has designed.

No matter how many times I cried out to the Lord to take away the pain, God's will for me at that time was to learn that in "worship" it means that I live according to His will. My heart was turning tender to the will of God to the point I could say though He slays me yet will I trust him. After thinking if I am a good wife meaning I would wash and iron clothes, cook food, clean the house, work full-time, see about kids, buy the kids what they wanted, keep the presentation of the house looking good from the outside, then I was doing something big in the Lord. That was not the vision God saw. Through a divorce that I did not ask for, my children living in a different city away from their mother, and a home with no one there, God showed me I was in the right place for Him to bless me and lift my worship gracefully. Don't get me wrong; I am not saying that all of this will happen to you, this is a part of my story, but whatever purpose God has for your life fully embrace the situations you must walk through. Jeremiah 29:11 tells us that God has a plan for our lives, plans to do us good and not evil, plans that will lift and not hurt; plans that will give us hope and a future. I am now seeing so many doors open for me that no man can shut. No matter how it may appear, I am walking with a servant's heart towards God. I am living my best life. I love how God transitioned me from worship that left me empty to true worship and what I thought I lost, was my gain. During my transition, I engulfed myself in going to revivals, studying the Bible, and praying each night to the Lord. I focused on doing my Father's business.

Today, I want nothing more than for God to be seen in me. Galatians 2:20 (AMP) - I have been crucified with Christ [that is, in Him, I have shared His crucifixion]; it is no longer I who live, but Christ lives in me. The life I now live in the body I live by faith [by adhering to, relying on, and completely trusting] in the Son of God, who loved me and gave Himself up for me. I can now say that I have a genuine heart of worship, and what I saw as lost is only my gain in the Lord. I am free, hallelujah graciously broken; I'm free.

You can be free too by choosing this day to open your heart to God and allowing Him to "Lift Your Worship Gracefully."

My Prayer For You:

Heavenly Father, Lord I thank You for what You have done in my life, and I know if You did this for me, You desire to do for others too. So, Father for each person reading this book, Lord walk thru the pages of their life. Take out those things that are holding them back or hindering them from moving forward in You. Lord, I thank You for giving Your life in exchange for every one of ours so that we can live a life full of grace and giving You glory in Jesus name, Amen!

CHAPTER 7

I Dare You To
Say Different

By Kimberly Pinkney

I Dare You To Say Different

By Kimberly Pinkney

"Oh man! Not another test; I always blank out; everything seems to go blank the moment that test hits my desk." These are the words that came out of my mouth so many times I can't even count. These words filled my mind. No matter how much I studied - and boy did I study hard - it seemed that I could not pass any major test. I made A's and B's on quizzes, but when it came to midterms and semester finals, my scores usually ranged from low Ds to F's. I often became upset and frustrated throughout the test. I turned in each test, knowing I had no chance of passing, but praying nevertheless for a miracle. At that moment, all the answers came like a tsunami, flooding back into my mind. I wanted to run back into the classroom, snatch my test from the teacher's desk and say, "I know all the answers now." But it was always too late.

In consultation after consultation, teachers and professors noted my ability to score well on quizzes, and yet my tendency to perform horribly on major tests. They marveled that I might have test anxiety...or something. I tried to explain the mental blankness I experienced only to be encouraged, rather tritely, to work harder. And yet, the next time, despite how hard I tried, the answers just did not come, at least not when it mattered. Thus, school itself became a bane to me: I happily started each year, anticipating a new and different beginning, until that first major test, which inevitably brought with it failure and despair. This constant barrage of torment continued for years. Unbeknownst to me, the enemy had encroached on my soul, little by little, until a stronghold had developed.

That stronghold came through words, and it presented quite a challenge to my academic success. We cannot escape words. They are thrown in our faces daily from the news media, through television shows, on our jobs, in our classrooms, through our phones, by the myriads of people we encounter in our lives. Words, good or bad, have a purpose, and you get to decide how they impact you.

Proverbs 18:21(MSG) states, Words kill, words give life; they're either poison or fruit - you choose.

The Amplified version of this verse says:

Death and life are in the power of the tongue, And those who love it and indulge it will eat its fruit and bear the consequences of their words.

If only someone had taught me this scripture when I was young, it would have saved me a lot of stress. Growing up, like most children, I heard all kinds of words: some good and some I wish I could erase from my memory. Yet, I had an enduring fascination with words, so much so, that I enjoyed looking up new words and using them at every opportunity - in conversation, in papers, in sermons, etc. Looking back, I believe that God was introducing me to the power of words, but I simply had no one to take me beyond this mere fascination. I attended my church three times weekly and heard sermons on godliness, positivity, business, and even soul winning. However, I do not recall one sermon on the importance of words, especially those that come out of one's own mouth daily. Later, I joined a Pentecostal church, met and married my husband, and moved with him to Germany on assignment with the Army. It was during this time I received a dose of deliverance that changed the course of my life. It was, indeed, a pivotal point in my life.

We had been married for only five days when my husband kissed me good-bye and boarded a bus to St. Louis Lambert International Airport to take a flight to Germany. To my delight, I joined Robert about a month later, a few weeks earlier than I had been told. A few days after my arrival, Robert began giving me the lay of the land. One thing he told me was to get a European driver's license, I would have to take two tests: a signage test, consisting of a hundred traffic signs involving picture matching; and a written test consisting of a hundred questions. Both tests required a passing score well beyond the average 70 percent.

Unlike driver's licensing tests in America, taking these tests required several hours.

Just hearing about these tests brought back unpleasant memories and quite a bit of consternation. After all, it had taken me several attempts to pass the written examination for my U.S. driver's license, which was allegedly easier than its European counterpart. My calm exterior veiled the nervous wreck I was on the inside. I was regretting having to take another test and worried that I would never be able to drive in Germany. As we saved money to buy a very used car, I began studying for the driver's tests, which involved reading, and trying to memorize, the contents of a very thick manual. I gave myself three weeks to get ready, and I studied every part of every page. I went over every sign, some of which were differentiated only by seemingly insignificant details. There was so much to learn, like converting miles to kilometers and German traffic laws. I made study notes, which I reviewed continuously, as well as flashcards and multiple-choice questions to quiz myself. I studied like my survival depended on it. I was determined to take this test only once.

One day as I was studying, a friend called me to inquire about my day. I told her that I was preparing to take the driver's test, and she was glad to hear it. With absolutely no prompting from her, I proceeded to tell her how my mind would go blank before taking tests. I told her I was studying really hard to try to keep that from happening. I was utterly oblivious of the fact that although I was preparing to pass the test by vigorously studying, I was assuring my failure with the words of my mouth. Fortunately, that point was not lost on my friend.

Her sweet, calm voice suddenly took on a stern tone when she rather loudly said, "You quit saying that!" "Saying what?" I countered. "Quit saying you always blank out on tests," she pressed. "But I do!"

I saw nothing wrong with stating things as they were. It never occurred to me to say anything different. My friend asked me what Philippians 4:13 (KJV) says, and I quoted it to her: I can do all things through Christ, which strengthens me." She went on to explain to me that the reason my mind kept going blank before tests were because I kept saying it would. I expected it to happen that way, and my expectations thus far had not been disappointed. She challenged me to say something different; to say Philippians 4:13 instead...to do so while I studied, thus creating a different expectation with my words.

I thanked her, and after hanging up the phone, I realized that had been my problem all along. I had been opposing God's Word with my words; I had merely been saying the wrong thing. Right then and there, I made a commitment to confess God's Word regarding my ability to pass this test. Every time before I picked up my study material, I'd say, "I can take and pass this driver's test through Christ, which strengthens me." I quoted this scripture throughout each study period, and I made sure to do it every time fear or doubt confronted me. Every time! I'd awaken in the middle of the night, with that scripture on my lips, because the enemy, as dirty and rotten as he is, would attack me with fear in my dreams. And I said it throughout the day even when not studying, in the shower, during housework, in the car - wherever and whenever! I must have said it hundreds of times.

One thing God revealed to me about words was that when you speak demonic words, words of fear, words of failure, or words that disagree with God, you build strongholds in your soul (your mind, will, emotions). To be victorious, we must destroy these strongholds. Demonic strongholds serve two purposes: they keep the wrong things in, and

101

they keep the right things out. They can even keep you from receiving the help that God brings you through others. The only thing that can destroy those strongholds and bring deliverance is the Word of God - absolutely nothing else! So, every time thoughts of doubt, fear, anxiety, pressure, or any other demonic idea whispered to my mind, I returned fire with Philippians 4:13.

Those words from Proverbs 18:21(AMP) - Death and life are in the power of the tongue, and those who love it and indulge it will eat its fruit and bear the consequences of their words - took on a greater meaning. The stronghold the devil had built in this area of my life came crashing down! And I was allowing the Word of God to create a new stronghold in my soul, one that expected to pass, not fail. One that brought me freedom from demonic influence and lies. And one that has kept me out of such bondages until this very day.

Having tasted freedom, I was determined never to return to this bondage. I was thoroughly persuaded of the ability God had put in me to pass tests. And no devil could sway me otherwise.

James 1:21admonishes us to humbly plant in our hearts the Word of God, which has the power to save our souls. This word save here means "heal, rescue, preserve." The scripture my friend ministered to me on that fateful day found its way into my heart and out of my mouth. It healed me from the hurt of past failures, rescued me from current failures, and preserved me from future failures. It utterly destroyed the bondage the devil had wielded over my mind for all those years. Hallelujah!

So, for weeks, I studied and confessed day and night. The day of reckoning - that is, the day of the test - arrived at last. I will admit that I was little nervous, but I kept quoting that scripture on my way to the test, as I walked to the testing site after I signed in, and as I waited to take the test. When the test administrator handed me the sign test, and I turned it over to begin, I was overcome with praise. I could see right away that the test was intact; I was not experiencing the usual mental blankness. I went through that test quickly, recognizing all the signs and matching them with their corresponding answers. When I turned in the test, the evaluator seemed alarmed that I had finished so quickly. His concern faded as he graded the exam, revealing that I had only missed two questions out of one hundred. Of course, I wanted to jump and shout.

I was so thrilled: one down and one to go. He handed me the other test and instructed me to go to another section of the room to take it. I looked over the sheet of multiple-choice questions, still confessing under my breath that "I can take and pass this driver's test through Christ, which strengthens me." It took me about an hour and a half to finish, my confidence at an all-time high during the entire ordeal. And I was right to be confident: I only missed three questions! In fact, at the end of the test, there were five questions regarding German Law, which I remembered from my studying. Initially, I was tempted not to pay attention to them because I just didn't think they would appear on the test. However, I studied them anyway and answered all of them correctly. The evaluator expressed surprise that I aced German Law, informing me that most people mess up on that section.

I received a temporary license and was told that a permanent one would be mailed to me later. I walked out of that office on cloud nine. I was thanking and praising God. I began shouting Thank You, Jesus repeatedly. I had passed the test. It seemed as much a spiritual test as a natural one. I had changed my way of thinking when it came to test-taking. I had consequently altered the words of my mouth and thus permanently altered my test-taking fate. Later at home, Robert called me from work, and I joyously gave him the good news! I also called my friend, told her I'd passed the test, and thanked her very much for her help! I called my mom and told her. I told everyone at church. This was an exciting day for me; it marked a significant turnaround in my life. And it was all because of the power of the Word of God. Hebrews 4:12 (AMP) puts it this way: "For the Word that God speaks is alive and full of power [making it active, operative, energizing, and effective]; it is sharper than any two-edged sword, penetrating to the dividing line of the breath of life (soul) and [the immortal] spirit, and of joints and marrow [of the deepest parts of our nature], exposing and sifting and analyzing and judging the very thoughts and purposes of the heart."

We returned to the States and eventually processed out of the Army. Years later, I decided to return to school to pursue a degree. With four children, I had a new outlook on life and school. I worked even harder and with greater confidence. And I received an Associate Degree in

Business Administration, graduating with a 3.8 GPA, and I confessed that same scripture throughout the two years it took me to get the degree. Since that time, I have applied this principle to every area of my life and have reaped countless rewards. In fact, this is the way Robert and I live and operate, and we have taught it to our children and to our congregation.

I want you to know that your victory over anything lies in your words. Your success or failure lies in what you speak every day. The devil will try to trick you and get you to say something different from the Word of God. For example, when the evaluator asked if I thought I'd pass the test, it was like the devil testing me to see if I really believed what I had been saying from the Word. Did I really believe that the Word had the power to change my situation or life enough to cause me to overcome anything I faced in life? You can count on him to test you in the same way. And with all the faith, nerve, and strength you have, you scream YES. No matter what it looks like, your words in agreement with God's Word will work every time!

The bottom line is that you play a vital role in the way things turn out for you. In fact, no one has a more significant role than you when it comes to securing your victory in every area of your life. So, you have a choice to make. Either you can either speak words of life that come from the living Word or the devil's words, which bring death and destruction. Joshua 1:8 tells us what happens when we make the Word of God our focus: "This Book of the Law shall not depart out of your mouth, but you shall meditate on it day and night, that you may observe and do according to all that is written in it. For then you shall make your way prosperous, and then you shall deal wisely and have good success." Joshua here highlights an essential purpose for meditating and speaking God's Word: it engenders obedience. When believers put their eyes on the Word and put it in their mouths, faith is released for obedience, which positions them for success in every area. How can you resist that?

Jesus is even more adamant in identifying the direct connection between your words and the reality of your life. For assuredly, I say to you, whoever says to this mountain, 'Be removed and be cast into the sea,' and does not doubt in his heart, but believes that those things he says will be done, he will have whatever he says (Mark 11:23 NKJV). This is not merely a promise; this is a spiritual law. It is a statement of truth; the way things really are. You will have whatever you believe in your heart and consistently say with your mouth. Years ago, this Law defined my ordeal with failing tests, and you can be sure that it describes your situation today. Again, everyone has a choice. There is no exception! People reap the consequences and fruit of their words, and there is no changing that.

God once told the Israelites something that applies to us as well: I have set before you life and death, blessing and cursing; therefore, choose life that both you and your descendants may live (Deuteronomy 30:19 NKJV). We clearly have a choice to make, and God has directed and empowered us to make the right choice - that is, the choice of life. Frankly, every decision you make, whether you realize it or not, is connected to either life or death. And choosing what you say is a crucial part of shaping the decision to choose life. Therefore, I admonish you to decide to speak right words - that is, align your words with the Word of God and speak them over your children, family, spouse, job, church, nation, leaders, and everything that pertains to your life, and watch God honor and bring His Word to pass for you!

If you have been speaking negatively, and your eyes are now open to the truth of your words, I want to lead you in a prayer of repentance and freedom.

Father, in the Name of Jesus, I repent for every negative word I have allowed to come out of my mouth. I repent for negative words I have spoken over my family, my spouse, my children, my job, my church, my leaders, my finances, and any other area. I command those words to die and fall to the ground and be destroyed. I declare crop failure right now over those words, in Jesus' Name. I realize the truth of your Word and how important my words really are. I declare this day that I will speak and sow seeds that bring life, prosperity, success, abundance, faith, and other words found in scripture. I believe that as I do this, I will reap good things. Father, I rely on the help of the Holy Spirit to guard my mouth and words and to lead me to repentance, as necessary. I believe, I receive, and I thank You and I praise You, Amen!

Go forth now in victory, knowing that it is a new day, and you have a new ground ready to produce your every Bible-compliant desire. When you sow seeds from His Word - that is, speak words that agree with His, and believe He will do it, you will reap an abundant harvest (Mark 4:20).

CHAPTER 8
Keep on Believing

By Darlenn Wilson

Keep on Believing

By Elder Darlenn Wilson

Many are the afflictions of the righteous, But the Lord delivers him out of them all.

Psalm 34:19 (NKJV).

"… Don't be afraid; just believe."

Mark 5:35-36 (NIV)

As many times as I have heard and read that scripture in Psalm 34, I did not know it could be like this. I thank God the scripture does not end at afflictions. It goes on to say, but my God shall deliver us from them all. Don't get me wrong, I was not naïve enough to think I would never have any problems in my life, I just did not believe they would be like this nor did I think I would have them all at the same time. Nevertheless, like the saints of old would say "BUT GOD."

As I reflect, back on this last year's journey of my life and the experiences I have lived through, I shout Hallelujah! Thank You, Lord, for keeping me. I give God all the glory for the opportunity to share how He allowed me to be gracefully broken for His honor and pleasure. Now I can bless Him for the stretching that took place in me for growth and the advancement of the Kingdom of God. Sometimes we want to stay complacent and in a comfortable position because it is tolerable and feels good to our flesh. I experienced trying times this past year in my health, relationships, on my job, and in my home. I

111

decided to get real with the Lord in my pain and confusion so that I could learn to trust Him even more during this season. If I had not gotten up and stopped the pity party, the wounds and the attack on my life would have taken me out.

As people of God, we must learn and become accustomed to embracing what the Lord allows to crucify our flesh so we will be able to serve Him with all our heart, soul, and strength. The Lord has a plan and purpose for each of our lives, and He needs you and me as a part of the body of Christ just as He needed the donkey and her colt to be loosed to serve the purposes of God in Jesus' Day (Matthew 21:2-3). The donkey and her colt had to be untied and brought to Jesus to fulfill their purpose that day. In the same manner, the Lord wants us to be untied from those things that hinder us and brought to Him so that He can equip us to fulfill His plan and purpose. The circumstances that occurred, which seemed insurmountable tried my faith in God and in His Word. My faith walk was tested, and the breath in me almost gave way to the experiences that confronted me so aggressively. I had to mentally and spiritually embrace "The Journey" the Lord allowed me to take so I would learn what it meant to walk by faith and not by sight (see 2 Corinthians 5:7). Family members, church members, nor any of my friends could do this for me. I had to make up my mind and be determined to say yes to the Lord with my whole heart, unequivocally.

I could not be ashamed or waiver about the decision I made. I said yes to the Lord, and there was no turning back, quitting, or changing my mind. I had to commit to the journey and go through the storms gracefully broken instead of complaining, murmuring, and being bitter. God promised that His grace would be sufficient for us and not our own strength

2 Corinthians 12:9 (AMP) states:

> ⁹but He has said to me, "My grace is sufficient for you [My lovingkindness and My mercy are more than enough - always available - regardless of the situation]; for [My] power is being perfected [and is completed and shows itself most effectively] in[your] weakness." Therefore, I will all the more gladly boast in my weaknesses, so that the power of Christ [may completely enfold me and] may dwell in me.

As an intercessor, I had to wake up and stop sleeping on the job. I had to get back to work and get it accomplished as the Lord called me to do and do it His way. The Lord was changing my prayer life and calling me to a higher place in my commitment to His purposes. He was allowing me to deal with the heart issues that had tripped me up for so long so I would finally be healed, delivered, made whole, and set free to serve Him no matter what anyone else had to say about the choice I made. I was bought with the price of the Blood of The Lamb of God (1Peter 1:18-19). I am His property, which was purchased and paid for in full (2 Corinthians 6:20; 1 Corinthians 7:23a). The Lord strengthened me. I was no longer bound or yoked to the old way of thinking and living. He healed my mind and restored my soul from past hurts and problems. God wants us to understand He calls and ordains us. He equips and provides for us, and sends us out for His glory. The enemy comes to steal, kill, and to destroy, but Jesus came to give us life in abundance and until it overflows in us and for us (John 10:10). The God we serve is Jehovah Roi. He sees and knows where we are in life. What occurs is never a surprise to Him. He promised never to leave us nor forsake us. Jehovah, God goes with us wherever life takes us (Deuteronomy 31:6). Make no mistake about it, our God is always aware of His children and their whereabouts. He is an awesome and caring parent to us! Amid her storm and chaos, in Genesis 16:13, Hagar gave this name to the LORD who spoke to her: "You are the God who sees me," for she said, "I have now seen the One who sees me." Hagar was an Egyptian slave who encountered God in the desert. Hagar ran away from her mistress Sarai because she treated her so harshly, but the Lord saw it all. God heard and saw Hagar in her distress and visited her in the wilderness. The circumstances created by her mistress afflicted her, but Jehovah Roi saw it all. There are times when we get in God's way and try to manipulate the course of our lives as Sarai tried to do using Hagar to give Abram a son. Sarai moved according to her own direction and not the promise of God made to Abram, but He knows what He is doing. God delivered Hagar, later fulfilled His promise to Abram, and Sarai bore her own child. We can rest assured that nothing happens to us that goes unnoticed by the Lord God Almighty. He is our Father. He will do the same for us as He did for Hagar, as we obey Him in all things and walk by faith.

As choose to live by our faith in God, refusing to give in to despair, doubt, fear, and what we see with our natural eyes, change begins to happen in us and for us. Romans 12:1-2 admonishes us to present our whole bodies to the Lord as a living sacrifice and be not conformed to the ways of this world. Let us be transformed and supernaturally changed by the renewing of our minds to live the God kind of life. John 15:5 (NKJV), states, "I am the vine, you are the branches. He who abides in Me, and I in him, bears much fruit; for without Me, you can do nothing."

We need God's spirit living on the inside of us to overflow to the outside, and onto others. We must bear fruit for God and be charged with His dunamis power to live the abundant life Christ came to give us. We are empowered to make a difference so others can see and desire to make the same difference in their world or sphere of influence. We must be confident in the Lord that what He has started in us He will complete it until Jesus returns. (Philippians 1:6). Be confident in the Lord, not in yourself or others (Psalms 27:3).

In the past, when I confronted trials, I put my confidence in people, things, money, titles, and what I thought I knew. Today, I am aware that all my help comes from the Lord (Psalms 121:2). I am fully persuaded that no one can help me as God can. I declare the Lord is my helper, strength, peace, battle ax, joy, hope, way maker, way out of no way, the rock of my salvation, shepherd, portion, refuge, fortress, high tower, provider, healer, deliverer, provision, and my great and exceeding reward. He is my God, the true and living God who is faithful.

Be encouraged and continue to believe God even when He allows you to be gracefully broken, knowing that He is positioning you for promotion and to greater work in His Kingdom and for His Glory. He gracefully and lovingly transforms us to fit the plan and purpose He has ordained for our lives. He is the Potter, and we are the clay. We must remain on the wheel until He is finished. Cry, wail, travail, and keep praying as the Holy Spirit leads, so you will know that the finished purpose of God is etched into your very being. The Bible lets us know in 2 Corinthians 12:9, God's grace is sufficient, and His power is made strong in our weakness. We must learn to allow the power of God to reign in us. Whatever it is He is calling you to release from your life, be obedient to do so. While going through many processes, I have learned that God knows what is best for me. He knows that what He orders, we will be faithful and do all to complete the assignment.

Mark 5:35-43 records the death of Jairus' daughter. Jesus was ministering to someone else before He arrived at the house to heal the synagogue leader's daughter. In the midst of the people lamenting her death, Jesus still encouraged her father to keep on believing. The servant had announced that the daughter was dead while also saying Jesus did not need to be bothered to come to the house. Jesus heard them talking to Jairus about the state of his daughter, but He ignored them and told the father of the young girl not to be afraid, only believe. Jesus says in John 11:25 (NLT), "I am the resurrection and the life. Anyone who believes in me will live, even after dying." When things such as marriage, family relationships, health problems, and money issues become lifeless and dried up, it is a test of our faith; we must draw closer to the Lord. God wants you to stand erect in what you believe without compromise and press into Him. Keep standing in the face of those things that appear to be dead. God alone will do and carry it out to fruition what He has promised. Whatever the Lord said to you, He will bring to pass. The Word of God lets us know that He is faithful and true. Keep believing when the circumstances say no. Keep believing even when everyone else says something different. Keep believing when we receive a poor diagnosis from a doctor's report. Keep on believing when we are being talked about and ridiculed for our faith. We must continue to stand strong in the Lord. We must continue to trust in God and not take down or back up. Our faith is in God and His Word! Trying and perilous times are here, and we must tighten up and stand fully clothed in the armor of God. Adverse circumstances do not dictate to the miraculous resurrection power of God! Psalm 62:11 declares that power belongs to God. In Ephesians 6:10-18, Apostle Paul admonishes us to stand strong in the Lord and in the power of His might fully dressed in the whole armor God supplies. Keep standing, keep on believing, keep persevering, keep staying faithful, and keep serving God and His people. Stay on the wall. Be like Nehemiah and declare you are doing a great work and you cannot stop, so keep praying and interceding for such a time as this!

My Prayer for You:

Father God, in the name of Jesus, I pray for the people who will read this book. May their lives be wholly transformed and renewed by the power of Your Word O' Lord. Let a fresh anointing fall on them to pray for their family, church, city, the lost, nations, and other believers as never before. I pray that as they read, people will be quickened in their spirit man to awaken and come alive to keep believing You in spite of what their circumstances may say and embrace what You are doing in them for this season. Father God, give them ears to hear what the spirit is saying to them. Give them ears to listen to Your instructions Father and the power to obey You. Bless them to be able to hear as moms, fathers, daughters, sons, intercessors, and ministers of the Gospel. Bless them with a heart that is receptive to embrace all you desire for them. Lord, help them not to shrink back or hang around any place You are calling them from. Grant them grace to say yes to You and Your will for their lives. Help them to come out of the pain, keep on believing, and keep praying as they are gracefully broken for Your glory in Jesus Christ Mighty Name, Amen.

WORLD INTERCESSORY NETWORK

Vision:

- To use prayer and fellowship as weapons to transform lives, unify and build the Body of Christ (1 Corinthians 12:12-26, Ephesians 6:18)

Purpose:

- To use both common and uncommon means such as electronic technology, book studies, teleconferences, fellowships, hands-on ministry and charitable acts of kindness to build and strengthen social networks among members of the Body of Christ (John 17: 20-23, Ephesians 4:1-16)
- To build camaraderie by admonishing Christians to think outside of the box and extend ministry beyond the four walls of local assemblies with the realization that every joint will supply.
- To host annual gatherings which will provide pastors, leaders, and Christians from various ministries throughout the world the opportunity for face-to-face fellowship.

Mission:

- Established in 2000, W.I.N. Inc. is a non-profit initiative comprised of experienced Christian leaders, prayer warriors, and intercessors who reside in various cities throughout the world. Our mission is to globally pray, build the Body of Christ and demonstrate His love through faith, fellowship, and servanthood. (James 5:13-16, Isaiah 62:6, Ephesians 4:11-12,1 Thessalonians 5:17, Luke 4:18-19)

Made in the USA
Columbia, SC
17 October 2022

69611146R00067